Practical Steps Toward Culturally Responsive K–12 Literacy Instruction

Practical Steps Toward Culturally Responsive K–12 Literacy Instruction

Resisting Barriers, Using Texts, and Making Space

Christy Howard
Mikkaka Overstreet
Anne Swenson Ticknor

ROWMAN & LITTLEFIELD
Lanham • Boulder • New York • London

Published by Rowman & Littlefield
An imprint of The Rowman & Littlefield Publishing Group, Inc.
4501 Forbes Boulevard, Suite 200, Lanham, Maryland 20706
www.rowman.com

86-90 Paul Street, London EC2A 4NE, United Kingdom

Copyright © 2024 by Christy Howard, Mikkaka Overstreet, Anne Ticknor

All rights reserved. No part of this book may be reproduced in any form or by any electronic or mechanical means, including information storage and retrieval systems, without written permission from the publisher, except by a reviewer who may quote passages in a review.

British Library Cataloguing in Publication Information Available

Library of Congress Cataloging-in-Publication Data Available

ISBN 978-1-4758-6458-8 (cloth)
ISBN 978-1-4758-6459-5 (paperback)
ISBN 978-1-4758-6460-1 (electronic)

We dedicate this book to all the educators who continue to believe and act in the pursuit of liberation, justice, and healing during these perilous times.

The purpose of education is not to bolster our egos, but to ensure that students feel self-empowered, self-reliant, self-determined, and self-liberated.

—Dr. Gholdy Muhammad

Contents

Foreword	xi
Acknowledgments	xv
Introduction	xvii
Chapter 1: Persevering through Challenges to Culturally Affirming Instruction	1
Chapter 2: Using Texts to Explore Identity, Community, Storytelling, and Standards	13
Chapter 3: Making Space for Culturally Affirming and Responsive Literacy Assessment	33
Chapter 4: It's Not "One More Thing": It's the Only Thing	51
References	59
Index	65
About the Authors	69

Foreword

To whom are your commitments? As a person? As an educator? Where do your loyalties lie?

Why? How do you know? What is your evidence?

Frequently when I speak to educators or parents about the work I do around LGBTQ+ inclusive literacy practices, the adults in the room are nervous. They worry that they don't know the right words, or that they'll inadvertently say the wrong thing, or that they don't know as much as the children they are hoping to serve and not to harm. They're right. The words are always changing and the youth will always know more than the adults. But that doesn't preclude us from trying.

When I was learning how to be a teacher in the 1990s, my professors frequently reminded the class that our students should not be expected to leave who they are at the door of our classrooms. While it seems that policy makers in the 2020s didn't get that message during their college years, Drs. Overstreet, Howard, and Ticknor bring readers back to that idea over and over in this brilliant text. However, unlike my professors or today's policy makers, these three scholars begin with us, the teachers. The first tenet of their framework is an examination of both self and systems. If my experiences leading professional development are any indication, educators who want to do right by the children they serve desperately need guidance through this tenet.

Culture is trying to help us. It might not *feel* like it, but when this book's authors reference Cardi B on page 34 of this volume, it hit home for me. We do not have to choose between two binaries or concepts or poles, we can do both. We do not have to choose policy over people, ourselves over our students, or, as I want to highlight in this foreword, who we are as teachers over who we are as humans. Going one step beyond my pre–No Child Left Behind professors, *nobody* has to leave themselves at the door of the classroom.

To whom are your commitments? Where do your loyalties lie? How do you know?

In order to do the work that the authors are asking educators to do, we must explore our own commitments. As I have written elsewhere (Hermann-Wilmarth, 2019), it would be impossible for teachers to share all, or even most, of the identities of our students. The authors of this volume caution readers against using deficit language when it comes to our students, but I do think it can be helpful for individual teachers to frame and then investigate our own deficits. As a white, cisgender, queer, English-only speaking teacher from a socioeconomically privileged background, what experiences of the world am I, personally, missing? What do the children and learners that I serve and want the best for know that I never can? And, how can I demonstrate that I want to center the experiences that I am lacking, or that the students whose power is diminished by the biases and policies made by those for whom, as Dr. Bettina Love (2019, 2023) reminds us, schools were built?

In order to teach in ways that center children against whom policies have worked while not feeling like this pedagogy is just one more thing on the already full plates of teachers, we have to investigate our own deficits. We have to read widely (the reference list at the end of this book is a great start), we have to resist interrupting/challenging/denying the experiences of people whose lives have been pushed to the margins by those who are more concerned with maintaining the wealth and power of some over the well-being and empowerment of most. And we have to center these experiences as we make textual choices, write lesson plans, and create opportunities for children to learn and tell us about the world we all live in so that their literacy skills reach all possible potential. We, as educators, have to do the reading and listening, show our work on our bookshelves and in our curricular materials, and do all of it without expecting a medal. Because it isn't one more thing. It's the only thing.

To whom are your commitments? Where do your loyalties lie? How do you know?

More recently, I have written about how community is key to sustaining a career as an educator who centers identity in one's scholarship and teaching (Hermann-Wilmarth and Ryan, 2023). While learning about lives that are different from our own requires us to look outward, finding sustenance for the work that this volume asks of us as educators requires us to look to others who are striving toward the same goals. Rather than processing difficult truths out loud, or with people who live those truths daily, educators should create solidarity with others who not only want to do the reading, but who want to change the system. When you know whom your commitments are to, and where your loyalties lie, find others whose vision of education and possibility for children aligns with yours. You will know, and they will, too, by the ways you are humble about your mistakes and lack of knowledge, the ways that you show your work, rather than tell your ideas, and how the communities you serve trust you with their precious children.

The authors of this text invite readers into relationships, action, and to move beyond diversity checkboxes. And they don't expect us to do it on our own. Their examples and ideas are laid out in the pages, but if we don't do our own internal work, their ideas will not exit the doors of our classrooms and enter the lives of children and communities. They want us to question how we have internalized messages about children and their communities, and implore us to help children write narratives about themselves that value their identities and brilliance. They hope that our voices will create a chorus of voices that support all children, no matter which children are in our classrooms, finding the wiggle room in sometimes rigid curriculum to build, maintain, and strengthen both relationships and pedagogy. By inviting us to be better teachers, they are also issuing an invitation to be better humans. Don't choose between being a great teacher to all of your students and living as a human with the integrity that values the humanity of all people. One requires the other. Do both.

Jill M. Hermann-Wilmarth

Dr. Jill Hermann-Wilmarth is professor of social foundations in the College of Education and Human Development at Western Michigan University and co-author of Reading the Rainbow: LGBTQ-Inclusive Literacy Instruction in the Elementary Classroom

Acknowledgments

Writing a book does not happen in a vacuum. We relied on many people, including each other, to support us through the process of writing a second book. We'd like to acknowledge and thank our families, colleagues, friends, students, and all the teachers we have worked with over the years who keep us grounded. Christy would like to thank Jeremy and Maya for being her late-night listeners when a day of writing and reflection kept her up at night. She would also like to thank Claire for being a caring, critical friend in this process, asking the hard questions from different perspectives. Mikkaka would like to thank Gary for helping her create a life that makes all of this worth the effort. Anne would like to thank Rob for always being her biggest supporter and Rachel Baker for helping her carve out time to write. We would also like to thank Meredith Hill, who provided early feedback on our manuscript and Bethany Early who provided her editorial expertise. We also want to thank each other for putting up with us, pulling us through, and reminding us why this book was needed.

Introduction

The epigraph at the beginning of our last book came from the brilliant educator Dr. Bettina Love as she reminded us that education could not save us, it was instead up to us to save education. We have taken up this notion with a greater sense of urgency and we continue to consider the ways in which culturally responsive instruction can work toward saving education. In our last book, *It's Not One More Thing: Culturally Responsive and Affirming Strategies in K–12 Classrooms*, we focused on the importance of knowing ourselves and our students as we created authentic lessons to enact culturally responsive instruction, emphasizing that we must go beyond the lessons and adopt a mindset of affirmation and validation as we work with K–12 students. As we ended that book, we reflected on the state of our country and the turmoil our nation was in as well as our desire to continue to "be better equipped for the ways in which our world continues to change" (Ticknor et al., 2021, p. 63).

Each day, change comes in ways that are detrimental for education and we are more passionate than ever to continue this work. We continue this journey understanding the harm education systems have caused and continue to cause, particularly for marginalized students. We recognize the good work already being done by so many educators as they teach through a culturally responsive lens. We hope this book will further assist people on their journey by offering practical ideas for implementation as well as support in our own journeys of self-work and the dismantling of harmful practices, policies, and curriculum. As of this writing, the governor of Florida, Ron DeSantis, has banned the new AP African American Studies class (*Good Morning America*, 2023) in the state of Florida citing it is "contrary to Florida law" and "lacks educational value." In addition to the push to erase the history of people of color, several states have also passed laws banning books and the inclusion of LGBTQ+ topics, not realizing that the erasure of people in history classrooms and on bookshelves does not negate the fact that we exist. We are still here. As we consider the words of Dr. Love and our roles in saving education, we must examine the harm education has done in our lives and the lives of our students and ensure that we do not further enact this harm. We must push against the erasure of humans and humanity and create classrooms where all students feel loved, validated, and affirmed.

Current laws and policies cause harm as students' experiences are devalued and erased in classrooms, but this is not new. Dr. Bettina Love's newest book, *Punished for Dreaming: How School Reform Harms Black Children and How We Heal*, gives an in-depth view into the historic educational policies and "reform" efforts in this country that pathologized and harmed Black children. Current research shows the racial discrepancies in discipline policies for students of color as well as the discrepancies in resources for schools serving mostly students of color (U.S. Department of Education, 2018). In addition, in many classrooms, marginalized students' experiences were absent from the curriculum and class community long before laws and policies were written censoring these topics. This is just the tip of the iceberg when we discuss educational harm. The harm that continues to ensue in pre-K through higher education classrooms is why this work is so imperative.

Often people tell us that we should not focus on culturally responsive instruction in the early grades. Our response is that the harm starts early for marginalized students, so we *must* start in the early grades. My (Christy) daughter was in preschool when she had her first negative experience related to her race. At four years old, she came home in tears because a little boy in her class told her he could not play with her because she was Black. As a mother, my heart broke for her because like many years of my own education, my daughter was the only Black student in her classroom and she did not realize the implications of being Black in predominantly white spaces. I knew this would be the first of many experiences that would bring her tears because of her identity. Through her tears, she said, "Mommy, I'm not Black, the seats in Dad's car are Black. Why would he say that? Why doesn't he want to play with me?" In that moment, I tried to comfort her, and I tried to explain to her that she was beautiful, worthy, important, and yes, Black. I tried to teach her how to advocate for herself as a beautiful Black girl at four years old, but in so many ways in that moment, I know I failed her. I should have told her these things prior to that day. I should have explained to her that being Black is wonderful and amazing, and something to be proud of, but I should have also warned her that not everyone would see her that way. I know her perspective of the world changed that day as she realized people would judge her based on her beautiful brown skin. There was no going back to yesterday when she could just "be" with her friends and learn and love them without fear of how they may reject her based on her physical features.

There was something else happening in that classroom, a teacher who did not stand up for my daughter at that moment, to tell the student who ostracized her that his behavior was not acceptable. Perhaps it was easier to say, "Go play" than to take a stand against racism. Perhaps the teacher felt it was her responsibility to remain "neutral," but her neutrality allowed the ignorance to continue and the harm against my daughter to permeate. What message does our silence convey?

Many years later, when my daughter was older and we were discussing the work I do around culturally responsive instruction and our journey with racial healing, we talked about that day and other experiences we had with racism, harm, and rejection in school. In that discussion with her, I could not help but wonder if her preschool teacher had been teaching through a culturally responsive lens, with books upon books around the classroom that showcased authentic experiences of diversity in race, culture, gender, religion, etc., would her experience have been different? What if her teacher taught her students to learn about and affirm the identities of themselves and others? What if her teacher believed in cultivating genius and unearthing joy (Muhammad, 2020, 2023)? Would my daughter have known there was nothing wrong with the beautiful brown hue of her skin? Would her classmates have known to validate and affirm each other and their identities in that space of classroom community? Would she have been spared the harm of rejection, isolation, and othering, which then led to insecurities, feeling "less than" and inadequate? I can't help but to think and believe if that preschool classroom had been taught through the lens of culturally responsive instruction, her experiences may have been different. Instead of creating harm, this space could have created validation and joy. So, no, I do not believe children are too young to be taught through a culturally responsive lens, particularly when some of them at the age of four are being taught to oppress, reject, and harm others because of their identity.

While I have also experienced harm at the hands of my teachers by being falsely accused of cheating as a second grader, being told I can't read the lines of the princess in the play we're reading in class because the princess has blonde hair, being blatantly denied help in class, even when I requested it, and so many other harmful experiences, I am not free of enacting harm as well. When I became a classroom teacher, I taught the way I was taught, and I taught the way I was taught to teach. This included using texts that were not representative of the lives and experiences of my students, upholding the biased discipline and tracking policies of the school and district, and failing to advocate for students when I should have done so. I share this from a place of shame, embarrassment, and regret as a Black woman. I have made many mistakes as an educator, but being able to recognize the harm I caused has been an important part of my own healing and excavation process. Muhammad (2020) has taught us that as we enter this work, "teachers must first do their own self-work. This work involves teachers deeply unpacking their own histories, identities, biases, assumptions, and tensions with racism and other oppressions they have learned, experienced, and practiced." As I come to this work, I have recognized the harm I have learned, experienced, witnessed, and practiced in education and I use this knowledge in my journey of healing and serving others through a culturally responsive framework.

While I recognize my responsibility as a parent and have sat with my "should haves" for many years related to this situation, I believe as a society and as educators we should have done a better job of teaching children not to discriminate because of the color of someone's skin, not to make others feel small and unwanted and to quite simply, not be racist. Further, I believe that when we see this behavior, we must be upstanders and not bystanders (Ahmed, 2018). We continue to try to help students navigate harmful, unsafe, unwelcoming spaces, when instead we need to reject, disrupt, and dismantle these harmful spaces in education and beyond.

I (Mikkaka) always loved and did well in school. For most of my elementary and middle school years, I was quiet, compliant, and hard working. While I was more vocal and outgoing in high school, I still stayed out of trouble and got good grades, eventually graduating as salutatorian of my class. I loved to read and to write and so excelled in those areas, but I worked hard to succeed even in the subjects that came less naturally to me. Because of this, I was usually well-loved by my teachers.

The harm that I experienced was in the ways my overachieving academic identity conflicted with other aspects of who I was. I was poor, Black, and from a "broken home"—an at-risk child who succeeded in spite of my home life. It was easy for my teachers to teeter between encouraging adults and white saviors. I knew what parts of myself to suppress and hide in order to be liked. I saw how they treated the other kids who rode the school bus with me from our "rough neighborhoods." The loud and boisterous behavior that was normal outside of school had no place in the halls and classrooms. I knew to carefully pronounce the sounds at the ends of words, to code switch when I stepped into the school building. I knew that much of my success in school was because I was not like the other poor Black kids.

Unfortunately, this expectation to choose between my culture and my education created a lot of tension and anxiety. I was an outsider, even among the most affectionate of my Black friends and family. I "talked white" and seemed weak and soft in comparison to my neighborhood peers. I was teased and picked on, like many kids, but that wasn't the worst of it. The worst part was always having to fracture myself to be accepted. No matter where I was, some part of me was wrong and had to be hidden away.

When I became a teacher, I was determined to teach kids like me and help my community. However, I ended up at an affluent, predominantly white school. There, I saw how my colleagues treated the two buses of poor Black kids. I heard the coded speech and witnessed the lowered expectations. I laughed along in the teacher's lounge as other teachers made fun of those students' unique names and lamented their parents' lack of involvement. Yes, sometimes I helped—intervening in matters of cultural misunderstanding and advocating for the kids when the other teachers didn't understand the underlying issues at hand, but I didn't do enough. Like Christy, I often taught the way I'd been taught, and the way I'd been taught to teach. I am ashamed by how many students I failed to stand up for, to fight for, to try harder to reach, to affirm and validate, and love as they deserved to be loved.

For me (Anne), harm came in the success and ease that I had as a student who repeatedly was given the benefit of the doubt. My grades were always good enough and I was able to move through my K–12 education, and some of my college education, with little effort. The harm I caused to others was unknown to me during much of this time, and it was much later when I realized that my educational successes caused harm and oppressed my peers as well as myself. Part of the reason I believe I was able to move through my early schooling easily was due to several factors that included my identities as a white, middle- to upper-class, traditionally feminine girl who smiled often, was sociable, active in extracurricular activities, and came from a family valued in the community. These identities positioned me to be perceived as able to be successful, even if I did not consistently demonstrate this, in school. I was smart enough to pass my courses, complete my assignments, and participate in class, but I did not excel. Yet I graduated high school and college and started to work as a teacher. It was during my experiences as a student teacher and then as a classroom teacher I realized the harm that I had caused and was perpetuating now as an elementary teacher in the biases I held about success and knowledge.

As a white fourth grade teacher in a predominately Hispanic serving elementary school in North Las Vegas, my (Anne) Midwest, monolingual, and mostly white educational experiences did not prepare me to enact culturally responsive and affirming pedagogies in my classroom instruction. As Christy and Mikkaka shared, I, too, taught as I was taught and as I was taught to teach. I was taught to enact a caring and nurturing approach to teaching, but it did not include examining my biases of success or reflecting on the representations of people and communities in my classroom materials nor in how I communicated with my students and their families.

I quickly learned that I was grossly inadequate at affirming the lived experiences of my students because I held misconceptions and biases that I had not examined. Yes, I had started to do this during my college experience when I sought out friends and experiences who had different identities than my own; however, I was just beginning this work, and was not overly successful, until a few months into my full-time teaching experiences. I remember clearly when a male-identifying student asked me if my precious classroom library had any "boy books" that he could read. Had I not considered gender when collecting books to have in my classroom? Certainly not in the way he had imagined or needed to engage him in reading. I also clearly remember sitting in one of my first conferences with the family of one of my students and realizing that if I wanted to communicate with this family, and many others in the community, I would need to learn how to communicate in Spanish. Sure, I had taken the requisite courses in foreign languages my high school and college required; however, as I described earlier, I got good enough grades but did not excel. I was given the benefit of the doubt because I smiled and engaged in class but I did not take learning a language other than English seriously enough to be able to communicate with the families of my future students. To be honest, I could not imagine I would need to use a language other than English in my future life and did not understand how important it would be to be able to communicate with others in their first language.

Finally, I saw the harm I enacted in my classroom when I reprimanded one of my Black students for behaviors deemed not acceptable in the classroom. The rules I had envisioned for my classroom, and the rules that I had followed in my own schooling, were not inclusive of the multitude of ways to communicate, bond, show emotion, and to interact with others nor did they affirm the identities of my students or provide an inclusive classroom environment for my students to thrive. Besides learning how to include my students in determining how we should interact with each other in our learning spaces, I also learned that I needed to unpack my own history with education (Muhammad, 2020).

When I work with educators, I share my experiences of inflicting harm, and perpetuating oppression because I am interested in demonstrating how I am continually learning from the harm that continues to linger in my memories. I want to be honest in how I learned to be a culturally responsive teacher as well as provide real experiences as models to educators in their own unpacking of histories, growth, and healing. I also want to be open about how I had to first recognize I had done harm to students both as a student and as an educator then how I choose to intentionally engage in learning how to do less harm. This can be a humbling process; however, the results I believe are worth it. Examining biases, misconceptions, and unpacking our histories with education enables us to teach through a culturally responsive and affirming lens.

We believe literacy can allow us to change the world. We believe through culturally responsive literacy instruction we can heal from the harm we have experienced and caused. We can disrupt injustice, oppression, and racism in education that persists because of the flawed historical portrayals of people of color in this country, because of deficit language that plagues descriptions of students of color, because of the policies that track Black and Brown students, placing them at higher rates in special education courses and suffering from increased rates of suspension, because of the tension between the "model minority" trope and the exponential increase in anti-Asian racism since the start of the COVID-19 pandemic, causing Asian American students to suffer hypervisibility and invisibility simultaneously (Lee, 2022). If as educators and preservice teachers we can examine these systems and our roles in these systems we can create culturally responsive spaces that disrupt these systems and instead validate and affirm all students. In order to do this, we have designed a framework that captures this approach. This framework gives us an opportunity to confront, unpack, and disrupt literacy instruction that fails to validate and affirm the lived experiences and identities of students in our classrooms.

Our framework has five major components. We believe that in order to begin this work we must engage in:

1. **Examining Self and Systems:** We must understand ourselves and the systems in which we are working to change.

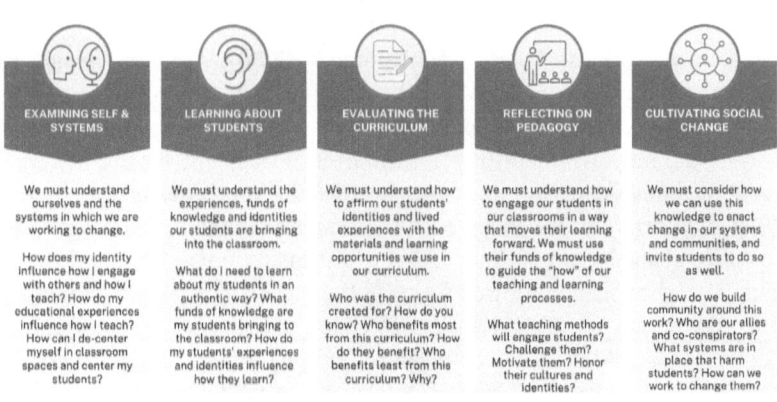

Figure I.1 Culturally affirming and responsive framework for transformative instruction: it's not one more thing.
Mikkaka Overstreet

2. **Learning About the Lives, Identities, and Experiences of our Students:** We must understand the experiences, funds of knowledge, and identities our students are bringing into the classroom.
3. **Evaluating the Curriculum:** We must understand how to affirm our students' identities and lived experiences with the materials and learning opportunities we use in our curriculum.
4. **Reflecting on Pedagogy:** We must understand how to engage our students in our classrooms in a way that moves their learning forward. We must consider how to do this effectively through lesson and assessment design, evaluating our language and practices, and by validating and affirming their identities, using their funds of knowledge to guide the "how" of our teaching and learning processes.
5. **Cultivating Social Change:** Understanding ourselves, our identities, and our curriculum and pedagogy is not enough. We must consider how we can use this knowledge to enact change in our systems and communities where needed and invite students to do so as well.

We must reflect on the knowledge of this framework as we continue to shift our lens to becoming more culturally affirming and responsive educators and through this knowledge, engage in action to incorporate more culturally responsive instruction.

EXAMINING SELF AND SYSTEMS

Through the work of Gholdy Muhammad (2020), Yolanda Sealey-Ruiz (2022), and Sara Ahmed (2018), we have taken up the importance of beginning this work with a critical examination of self. We must do the self-work of unpacking our own identities first. In order to do this, we are in constant reflection about our own experiences with education, racism, trauma, and healing. Collectively, we engage in discussions related to how our experiences have shaped and continue to shape our instructional decisions.

This work has been amplified for us in the years since the pandemic began and the continued senseless murders of Black people such as George Floyd, Breonna Taylor, Ahmaud Arbery, and countless others. As educators, we began to explore even further the role of our biases, beliefs, and experiences in an effort to unpack the "tensions with racism and other oppressions" we have "learned, experienced, and practiced" (Muhammad, 2020, p. 78). So powerful is this quote from Muhammad, to me as a Black woman (Christy). Her work also leads us to consider the historical perspectives of these tensions with racism and the current contexts in which we teach and the contexts we create as educators. We have learned to further explore the systems that were created steeped in racist policies and oppression and how our identities influence how we engage in these systems. We recognize we have to go beyond ourselves in this work as we continue to disrupt these systems by examining ourselves alongside the current structures within these smaller and larger contexts of education.

Our examination of self considers how we show up for students specifically as educators. Examining our identities means examining our personal experiences in school and outside of school. We also look at systems in place such as discipline policies, tracking policies, school assignment policies, district policies, general school "rules," deficit language guiding these systems, etc. In this work, we consider what it means for what and how we teach literacy with the goal of validating and affirming our students as they engage in the learning process. We have engaged in these conversations over the years through conversations, lesson planning, literacy research, writing, and personal reflection. We have asked ourselves, how does my identity influence how I engage with others? How do my educational experiences influence how I teach? How does my identity influence how I teach? Which parts of my identity do I need to explore more? How can I de-center myself in classroom spaces, and center my students? What systems are in place to support all students based on their identity? What systems are in place that hinder the success of students based on their identity? What is my role in these systems?

We understand this process of examining self and systems is ongoing and forever changing and we must continue to reflect and consider how we can enact change as well.

LEARNING ABOUT OUR STUDENTS

We believe that before we can actually teach our students, we must know our students. The beginning of the year surveys that ask our students what they enjoy doing outside of school, the last book they enjoyed, etc. mean nothing if we put a checkmark on them and put them away in our files. We have been guilty of this ourselves, but over time we have come to realize that how we use this information can be a great contributor to how we begin creating culturally responsive literacy classrooms.

Our students come to us with rich cultural experiences and funds of knowledge that are incredible assets to our classrooms. Creating safe classroom communities for students to share their experience and knowledge is imperative. It is important to understand the knowledge our students have and consider how we can validate and affirm this knowledge. We also must consider the knowledge we hope students will gain and how we can help them make connections between this knowledge and new literacy learning.

We have to provide opportunities for students to share their in-school and out-of-school interests and experiences and invite them into the discussion of learning goals. What do I need to learn about my students and how do I do this in an authentic way? What do our students want to learn more about in our classrooms? How do we engage with and support students based on their identities? What funds of knowledge are my students bringing to the classroom? How do my students' experiences influence how they learn? How do my students' identities influence how they learn?

This process takes time; it should be a part of our consistent community building. It's not simply a first day or first week of school activity. We then use this knowledge to develop a curriculum that meets the social, emotional, personal, and academic needs of students. We do this in order to provide multiple pathways to student success, validating and affirming their experiences and funds of knowledge, as opposed to seeing these components through a deficit lens. Throughout this book, you will find many examples of how we learn about our students and use this knowledge to address required standards while teaching through a culturally responsive lens.

EVALUATING THE CURRICULUM

As we consider the role of curriculum in our framework, we recognize the demands put on teachers to teach certain programs or required curriculum. We understand that freedom and autonomy are not provided in all school contexts, and, if this is the case for you, we want to encourage you to be critical consumers of the curriculum you are required to teach. In our work evaluating curriculum, we encourage teachers and school and district leaders to research the curriculum. Who was it created for? What students benefit most from this curriculum? What types of assessments are being offered? Do assessments give multiple options for students to showcase knowledge? Do the assessments amplify the brilliance of students? What types of knowledge are these assessments valuing? Does the curriculum consider student identity, community, and experiences? Does the curriculum center the lives of students?

There is so much to consider and it is not enough to accept the curriculum handed to you. Asking these questions and conducting curriculum audits can benefit your students and provide them with meaningful, culturally responsive experiences. If your curriculum is not beneficial for all students, we encourage you to use research to advocate for new curriculum materials. You can advocate that your students be represented in the curriculum and we encourage you to consider how you can supplement required curriculum materials with culturally responsive materials. As you read each chapter of this book, consider these questions: Can all students benefit from the ideas, lessons, and processes related to curriculum in this book? Do the ideas, lessons, and processes related to curriculum in this book consider the identities, communities, and experiences of all students? We hope your answer is a resounding yes.

REFLECTING ON PEDAGOGY

Reflecting on and evaluating how we teach is essential in our journey to become culturally responsive educators. Long gone are the days of sitting in rows and listening to teachers lecture. As we evaluate how we teach, we must evaluate our thinking around teaching and how this mindset permeates everything we do in our classroom, from assignment design, opportunities for engagement, assessment, etc. As educators, the three of us are consistently reflecting on how we teach in classrooms and in professional development sessions. We are analyzing the opportunities we provide for students and reflecting on how these opportunities connect to students' experiences, culture, and identities. We are consistently reflecting on how we present information and how we ask students to present their learning, understanding there are multiple avenues to learning and showcasing knowledge.

With this in mind, we teach with a range of resources. How we choose resources is just as important as how we choose our teaching methods. We must consider these components with our students in mind. What teaching methods will engage them? What will challenge them? What will motivate them? What will honor their culture? We must consider how we ask students to engage in learning processes. Will we ask them to conduct interviews? Observe people or places? Write creatively? Conduct experiments? Do we embrace the use of multiple languages in the teaching and learning process? Do we embrace multiple perspectives? In our examination of our pedagogy, we want to ensure that we are providing opportunities for students to explore their own cultures and cultures other than their own. As literacy educators our pedagogical practices include analysis of texts in ways that ask students to consider biases, stereotypes, representation, and cultural contexts while simultaneously meeting required expectations of literacy standards. All of these pieces are part of the evaluation process as we examine our teaching practices. Over the years, we have done this evaluation collaboratively with each other, observing our teaching, providing feedback, and offering ideas. These ideas are showcased throughout this book as well.

CULTIVATING SOCIAL CHANGE

We recognize that it is not enough to know what it means to be a culturally responsive educator; along with this knowledge must come action. As we collaborate in this work and find ourselves reflecting on our new knowledge, we are always left with the question, "So what?" What does this mean for how we will change our practices? How will we enact the beliefs we share? How will we engage in social change? First and foremost, we know that we do this work together and we do this work with the understanding that none of us are "all knowing." We are all learning. Together. In 2018, Dr. Bettina Love spoke at our university and as always, her message was powerful, her delivery profound. We were captivated by her urgent message around antiracist education. She left a lot with us that day, but one of her final points was to remind us that we don't have to do this work alone. The three of us were already working together in collaborative teaching, observation, and research, but these words from Dr. Love ignited that desire even more. We were also driven to evaluate our actions and what we were doing beyond focusing on a culturally responsive literacy lens in our classrooms.

Part of our action and "doing" is to revise our courses and assignments to better meet the needs of our students. We encourage social action on the part of students as well. We also ask ourselves how we can collaborate with students and the community. We listen as inservice and preservice teachers tell us they may not be able to teach through this lens because they have scripted curriculums or they are afraid of parent or administrative pushback. In the current climate where laws are preventing teachers from teaching about history, race, gender, and important social issues, we have to help preservice and inservice teachers be and feel confident, knowledgeable, and safe in teaching about topics related to diversity. We can do this work by continuing our research, talking with superintendents, principals, school boards, and families about the importance of equitable instruction. This work cannot end in our classrooms. Therefore, part of our action is to educate beyond the classroom. Collectively and individually, we have participated in learning exchanges with superintendents, provided professional development to media specialists and school leaders, and participated in literacy panels sharing knowledge about how to teach through a culturally responsive lens. We have been invited to speak by national organizations on this topic and share resources with others about how to do this work. We have conversations with superintendents and principals about why this work is important and how they can support their teachers and students. We recognize that action is a necessity and we take Dr. Bettina Love's words to heart and recognize that we cannot do this work alone.

As Bettina Love (2019) has written and shared in her talk at our university, we need co-conspirators: people who are committed to engaging and supporting each other to change education through action. Finding others who are committed to disrupting education is essential. As we have recently witnessed in our state and across the nation, affirming marginalized identities in education is being challenged with policies, laws, and actions. More books are being challenged, what constitutes reading instruction is being questioned, and curriculum materials are being scrutinized in an increasingly frenzied fashion. As educators committed to this work, having co-conspirators can lessen the isolation and bolster strength to continue enacting culturally responsive pedagogy and affirm all students.

As we conclude this introduction, we want to revisit and share our definition of culturally responsive instruction. We utilize the term "culturally responsive" because as Gay asserts:

> Culturally responsive teaching can be defined as using the cultural knowledge, prior experiences, frames of reference, and performance styles of ethnically diverse students to make learning encounters more relevant to and effective for them. It teaches to and through the strengths of these students. (2010, p. 31)

Though Gay focuses explicitly on race, culture, and ethnicity, she invites scholars to define diversity for themselves. Gay states that others "may focus instead on gender, sexual orientation, social class, or linguistic diversity as specific contexts for actualizing general principles of culturally responsive teaching" as long as they "make their commitments explicit and how they exemplify the general principles and values of teaching to and through cultural diversity" (2013, pp. 52–53). In our work we seek to make our commitment explicit as we focus on validating and affirming the students we encounter each day.

In this introduction we also want to remind you that in addition to our framework, we have guiding principles that keep us aligned with our beliefs about culturally responsive instruction and guide our work throughout this process.

Finally, we want to extend our heartfelt gratitude to you for continuing this journey with us. In this second book we will build on the guiding principles that were established in *It's Not "One More Thing"* and share learning through our framework. We extend the practical how-to strategies for enacting culturally responsive and affirming literacy instruction in K–12 classrooms. In this book we focus on strategies for culturally responsive and affirming instruction specific to literacy assessment, connecting identity,

GUIDING PRINCIPLES

- **Culturally responsive instruction is not one-size-fits-all.** By definition, this type of instruction is contingent on context. You cannot and should not pick up the lesson examples in this book and deliver them directly to your students. You must make considerations for the unique contexts in which you teach and learn and instead take up the principles guiding this work.
- **Culturally responsive instruction is not activities.** One cannot simply do our suggested activities and consider their instruction to be culturally responsive. You must also "do the work." This means changing your ways of thinking about teaching and students, engaging in deep reflection, and committing to a lifelong learning process of staying current on appropriate and affirming language choices, issues of equity, and societal trends.
- **Culturally responsive instruction is not just for "those" kids.** This is for everyone. All of our students deserve to be properly prepared to live in a diverse world. Affirming their cultures does not mean that you only teach this way if you have "diverse" kids in your classroom. Diversity is far more than what you can see, for starters, and so you must expand your thinking. Further, this work requires a disruption of traditional teaching, which is rooted in white, cisgender, Christian, abled, heteronormative, middle-class ideals. This has to be done in *all* classrooms so that *all* children can see themselves *and* others as a valid and valued part of the curriculum.
- **Culturally responsive instruction is not "one more thing."** This isn't an add-on or one more entry on teachers' already long to-do lists. Culturally responsive teaching is a method, a lens, a frame through which all of your teaching passes. You don't set aside a block of time for culturally responsive teaching, you do it all day; math, literacy, science, social studies, art, physical education, music, and all other subjects can and should be taught in culturally responsive ways and with a culturally responsive intentional way of thinking.

community, and storytelling, and navigating educational barriers. The book content is based on our experiences as K–12 teachers, teacher educators, and literacy researchers.

Introduction

Similar to our last book, we begin the next three chapters by sharing vignettes of literacy instruction that may be common in K–12 classrooms. We offer these examples as a way to situate how teachers may be using research-based and effective literacy practices while ignoring the identities and experiences of their students. Then we offer an overview of theories and concepts that are often related to culturally responsive teaching specific to literacy instruction in each vignette. We then disrupt the vignettes using the theories and concepts presented in the chapter to make visible how each practice could be reimagined to integrate more culturally responsive strategies. In this discussion, we highlight how we prepare teachers to recognize common, yet culturally irrelevant, K–12 classroom literacy practices. Our intent is that readers will see examples of how they may make more visible similar practices in their specific teaching contexts. Next, we present practical applications we have recently implemented in our literacy instruction. Finally, we offer guiding prompts for readers to use the chapter topic and examples to consider ways to be more culturally responsive teachers for their students and in their local communities.

In the first chapter, Mikkaka explores common barriers teachers may face when enacting culturally affirming literacy instruction and offers ways to persevere through these challenges. In the following chapters, each of us took the lead to offer readers a more personalized take on each of the concepts in our book and how we utilize the framework in our work with educators to offer practical applications. As with all of our chapters, our goal is to provide readers with ideas for practice; however, in no way are we hoping readers implement our ideas without first considering how the concepts can be adapted to fit their educational context. In the second chapter, Christy leads us through a journey of using texts to explore identity, community, storytelling, and standards. And in the final chapter of our application chapters, Anne takes us through ways to make space for culturally affirming and responsive assessments in our already packed days with K–12 students. We hope our readers see the clear connections to our framework in each chapter and see how our voices come together in the introduction and conclusion chapters. We wrote those together and were intentional in both pulling out our own identities and lived experiences, as well as combining them into a cohesive narrative about how we enact our commitment to equity in community with each other.

As you begin your journey with us through our second book, we hope you will benefit from this text in several ways. First, it will provide readers tangible ways to include more culturally responsive teaching in their literacy instruction. Second, it will provide readers with tools to support their instructional decisions in terms of literacy assessment, connecting identity, community, and storytelling, and how to navigate educational barriers. Third, readers will have an inside look at how we make instructional decisions based on tenets of culturally responsive teaching. Fourth, readers will be supported in their culturally responsive teaching decisions with self-reflection questions and prompts to support their teaching. Fifth, we hope you feel supported in a community of co-conspirators as you continue your journey to becoming a more culturally responsive and affirming educator and are provided ways to enact social change.

STOP AND REFLECT

1. How do you show up for your students in a way that validates and affirms their identities?
2. Muhammad (2020) says we should unpack our histories. What are your experiences with education? What are your experiences with literacy education? How has education served you well? How has education historically served people who look like you well? How has education not served you well? How has education historically not served people who look like you well?
3. How does your current curriculum consider student identity, community, and experiences?
4. What are the multiple opportunities you give students to showcase their knowledge on assignments and assessments?
5. How do you enact your beliefs?

Chapter 1

Persevering through Challenges to Culturally Affirming Instruction

SCENARIO 1: SMALL GROUP READING INSTRUCTION WITH MRS. NICHOLS

Mrs. Nichols teaches first grade at a school that serves a racially and linguistically diverse population. Despite having a high number of multilingual learners, her school does not provide English as a Second Language (ESL) supports, as families who attend the school opt out of such services. Each morning, the children gather to read with their teacher in small groups. Mrs. Nichols's first two groups are made up of students who need more intensive support. After the first group talks about their last book and share who they read to at home, they review sight words from their new text, locating the words as they preview the book. Finally, they begin to read as Mrs. Nichols listens in. Quietly, one Latinx, one multiracial, and two Black children read the story of a white girl named Meg and her cat that will not come down from a tree. Next, Mrs. Nichols calls a small group of two. She spends a lot of time talking about the text before they begin because both boys are multilingual learners who have difficulty reading. Caden is Vietnamese. Emmanuel is Mexican. They read about two white boys named Sam and Jesse and their day at the park.

SCENARIO 2: WRITING INSTRUCTION WITH MX. EDWARDS

Mx. Edwards teaches down the hall from Mrs. Nichols. They chose their school purposefully, wanting to work with a diverse student population.

1

While their white, middle-class identity is different from the racial and socioeconomic backgrounds of their students, they try hard to connect with students' lives and cultures. Autumn in their school district means it's time to write personal narratives. Mx. Edwards confers with their students, helping them brainstorm potential topics for their pieces. They model examples to the whole group, using mentor texts to demonstrate the elements of a good personal narrative. Still, many students have trouble coming up with topics. One such student is Caleel. Caleel comes from a large family that lives below the poverty line. When Mx. Edwards worked with Caleel to brainstorm topics, Caleel suggested writing about cooking dinner with his mother. Mx. Edwards encouraged him to think of something more exciting, but Caleel didn't volunteer any further ideas. Eventually, he wrote a story about riding a tiger. Mx. Edwards praised him for writing a story with several complete sentences and a clear beginning, middle, and end.

Mrs. Nichols and Mx. Edwards represent how educator's professional goals often have to change due to new barriers and challenges in their professional lives. They grapple with revising curriculum to meet new state literacy standards and interpreting what the standards meant for curricula, materials, assessments, and other teaching expectations. Balancing the interpretations of multiple stakeholders with the needs of the individual students in their classrooms, many teachers abandon lessons that they know will better serve their students because they are pressed for time and pulled in too many directions, leading to feeling exhausted or burned out. This chapter aims to offer practical ways to overcome barriers and enact our framework components: examination of self, understanding students, evaluating curriculum, and evaluating pedagogy.

Teaching is a challenging job. Teachers educate students while often dealing with multiple outside entities that question the teachers' intelligence, commitment, and motives (Finn, 2009). Teaching in the twenty-first century is a top-down profession; teachers often operate within mandated curricula, prescribed texts and basal programs, and on a school or district-wide schedule as dictated by the enforced use of pacing guides. Their students are evaluated by standardized assessments that are publicly used to rate their schools. Teachers are often almost powerless to do anything but comply with instructional decisions made by people outside their classrooms. According to a 2021 report from Pen America, "between January and September 2021, 24 legislatures across the United States introduced 54 separate bills intended to restrict teaching and training in K–12 schools, higher education, and state agencies and institutions" (Friedman & Tager, 2021, p. 4). Legislation is only one avenue for restrictions, as schools have also faced an unprecedented number of book challenges and bans (Pendharkar, 2022). The topics most often prohibited are related to race, racism, sexuality, and gender identity. Under such extreme pressure and tight restrictions, how are teachers to make decisions that deviate from the prescribed curriculum in order to meet the needs of a diverse student body?

BARRIERS AND CHALLENGES TO CULTURALLY RESPONSIVE AND AFFIRMING INSTRUCTION

There are many very real barriers obstructing teachers, but there are also cracks in these barriers, if we're brave enough to look for them. For example, some standards seem to limit teacher autonomy and culturally responsive teaching efforts, but actually allow room for pushback. While the current push is around the science of reading (SoR), a few years ago, this tension was felt with the Common Core State Standards (CCSS). These standards provided a baseline for what students need to know and be able to do in reading, writing, listening, speaking, language, and mathematics in order to be ready to attend college or pursue a career (National Governors Association Center for Best Practices [NGA] & Council of Chief State School Officers [CCSSO], 2010). These standards instructed teachers *what* to teach, but not *how* to teach it. So, while they must, for instance, teach students the necessary skills to "ask and answer questions about key details in a text" (NGA & CCSSO, 2010, p. 11), the standards do not mandate particular texts, questions, or methods for doing so.

In some states, teachers use materials adopted by the school's Site/School-based Decision-Making Councils (SBDMs)—groups composed of teachers, administrators, and parents. General practice sometimes dictates that schools consider the materials that are popular within the district and select from those, but schools often have the freedom to conduct their own research and use their own discretion. Still, many schools and districts embrace whatever programs are prevalent and popular at a given time. Such programs often provided scripted lessons to accompany the texts, which provide questions and activities for teachers to use with students. Many of these programs claim alignment with the standards and research of the day. However, simply because the sticker on the box says it's aligned to CCSS or SoR, it doesn't mean that the program inside the box is actually high quality or meets the needs of the diversity of individual classrooms. This is why it is essential that educators carefully evaluate their curricula.

As we emphasized in our last book, literacy education is an ideal setting for engaging in culturally responsive pedagogy (CRP). Ladson-Billings calls CRP a "pedagogy of opposition" that is built on collective empowerment

(1995, p. 160). It requires that students experience academic successes, develop cultural competence, and "develop a critical consciousness through which they challenge the status quo" (Ladson-Billings, 1995, p. 160). Students build self-esteem, engage in personally meaningful learning, *and* are held to rigorous academic standards. They do not just feel good about who they are, they learn, and they think critically.

Considering the research indicating that learning takes place when the content and delivery are meaningful and relevant to the life of the learner, a disconnect between culture and instruction is problematic. The curriculum is meaningless if the child is unable to connect to it. Students come to the classroom with preconceptions, knowledge, and experiences that teachers must access. As Muñiz (2019) uses Bishop (1990) to explain:

> Central to culturally responsive teaching is the belief that students' cultural background is a resource to learning . . . [C]ulturally responsive teachers plan learning encounters that validate students' lived realities, cultural identities, and heritage. . . . [They] strive to evaluate all textbooks and instructional materials they use to ensure they do not perpetuate stereotypes or fail to represent diverse groups. They complement the traditional curriculum with examples, newspaper clippings, articles, song lyrics, plays, comics, video games, and other resources that reflect experiences, characters, settings, and themes their students can relate to. They deploy *cultural scaffolding* by providing links between academic concepts and the experiences that are familiar to students. In addition to providing "mirrors" reflecting students' familiar world, teachers provide "windows" into the history, traditions, and experiences of other cultures and groups. (pp. 13–14)

DISRUPTING THE READING SCENARIO

Though educators might not always have access to materials that reflect their students' identities, there are ways to find such materials. With the internet and its multitude of resources, teachers have access to all manner of e-books, videos, articles, educational games, virtual manipulatives, and so much more. The local public library can be a treasure trove. They often stock multicultural and dual-language texts, audiobooks, DVDs, and other instructional materials. With a free library card, a patron can check out a great deal of material at a time and can even renew these items online, allowing educators to supplement their classroom materials with more diverse texts.

For example, I (Mikkaka) supported one of my preservice teachers, Anya, in teaching a unit she'd planned during my literacy methods course. During the unit, the class explored multicultural variations of the Cinderella story, which Anya checked out from the public library. She had the students compare the stories, study the countries they hailed from, and write about what they learned. Anya and her mentor teacher were amazed by the quality of the students' work and by the socio-emotional benefits as well. When given the opportunity to write about which of Cinderella's countries of origin they'd like to visit, several students selected Egypt because they'd learned that their classmate Nameera could speak Arabic and they wanted to hear her speak the language. After the unit, Nameera began to proudly wear her hijab to school, even though she explained she didn't have to wear it until she was older, and taught her classmates bits of Arabic. When Anya brought student's cultures into the curriculum, students began to value their own and their peers' funds of knowledge.

Anya's Cinderella unit was an example of applying CRP. The results were remarkable: the students met the standards, exceeded the mentor teacher's expectations for first grade performance, and succeeded socially and emotionally in unexpected ways. Usually quiet and shy, Nameera was inspired to openness by the recognition of her culture, opening spaces for interaction between her and her peers and building "a familiarity with each other, a shared purpose, and the seeds of friendship" (Case, 2015, p. 380).

DISRUPTING THE WRITING SCENARIO

Culturally affirming instruction takes time and teachers live on a stringent clock. There are only a finite number of instructional days allotted to cover content. Consequently, school leadership often mandates curriculum maps dictating when classes should cover certain material (and when they should be finished covering it, regardless of student mastery). In this environment, getting twenty-five to thirty first graders to complete coherent personal narratives has the added pressure of a time limit.

The CCSS required students have opportunities to communicate across the various modes of writing; this includes composing narrative, argumentative and informational texts in various forms and genres over time. Within narrative writing, students write both real and imagined narratives, which teachers generally interpret as personal narratives and short stories. The two types of narrative require different skill sets: one calls for the ability to relate an event that really happened in such a way as to make it clear and engaging for a reader, the other necessitates creativity in inventing characters and events.

Mx. Edwards's interactions with Caleel illuminated their beliefs about students like him—students with very different lives than their own. Though Mx. Edwards may try to reject deficit perspectives of students and families, they were unable to view Caleel through any other lens than that of their own values and culture. To middle-class adults, students whose life experiences consist of making dinner with mom might seem pitiable in comparison to their own upbringing. Most anyone with a compassionate spirit would be moved by Caleel's situation. However, it was Mx. Edwards's actions and not their feelings that were most important.

Mx. Edwards clearly has a desire to help underserved communities. However, such desires and the word choices associated with them, often carry deficit perspectives. Many educators use terms such as "at-risk," "urban," "those kids," and "inner city" as educational code words that imply deficiencies. I (Mikkaka) regularly work with districts who want to focus on *all* kids and avoid terms like "equity" or even "social-emotional learning." This is far too similar to a colorblind ideology, which is especially problematic since "the combination of claiming not to see skin color and then expecting students of color to be inferior prevents schools from providing the culturally responsive teaching that students need" (Winn & Behizadeh, 2011, p. 153). Instead, these students receive a "watered-down," remedial, test-driven, and skill-based education, unlike the "pedagogy of opposition" that Ladson-Billings (1995) advocates. All students deserve high quality instruction based on high expectations. Essential to this type of teaching is a challenging curriculum that accurately reflects the students being taught.

Mx. Edwards's feelings of pity toward Caleel reflected in their treatment of him in the classroom. Though they claimed to hold all of their students to high standards, when Caleel had trouble with the personal narrative assignment, Mx. Edwards changed their expectations, allowing Caleel to write an imagined narrative. He was no longer expected to meet the standard and, consequently, was denied access to valued mainstream knowledge. Further, his own life experience was devalued; he was considered to have no experiences worthy of being written about or shared with others. The personal narrative is one of few traditional assignments that obviously lends itself to CRP as the assignment intrinsically centers on the student. Perhaps if Mx. Edwards was unable to coach him through his own memories, they could have reminded him of shared experiences. In first grade alone he had dealt with the uncertainty of the first day of school, been on field trips, and attended class parties. In writing about these, Caleel could have met expectations while still seeing himself as a valued part of the curriculum.

Culturally responsive teaching involves creating a space in which school and home spaces overlap meaningfully and learning is connected to the real lives of students. You cannot have culturally responsive teaching without attending to the literate lives and home literacy practices of students. Family defines much of the culture of a person, thus if you are going to be responsive to a person's culture in your literacy instruction, you must have an awareness of, respect for, and understanding of the literacy practices of their family. Students' home languages, cultures, and ways of knowing should be authenticated and valued alongside school practices. Such teaching "utilize[s] students' culture as a vehicle for learning," capitalizing on the skills, knowledge, and interests of the students as a bridge to school learning (Ladson-Billings, 1995a, p. 161). This is the type of instruction Caleel needed from Mx. Edwards—instruction where the goal is empowerment through questioning, analyzing, and opposing inequities maintained by the status quo. When the school environment connects with the literacy practices of students' home lives, students from underrepresented populations may find themselves better able to create academically literate identities without feeling as if they must sacrifice their cultural identities to do so (Ladson-Billings, 1992).

Freire (2000) maintains that there exists a "pedagogy of the oppressed"—a system in which economically disadvantaged learners are given inadequate educational opportunities, leaving them ill-prepared for careers that would allow them to rise up and join the ranks of the middle class. In essence, this mirrors the familiar construct of the haves and the have-nots; the system operates in such a way that the status quo is maintained. While I would never accuse teachers like Mx. Edwards of consciously dooming their students to failure, it is imperative that educators recognize how marginalized populations have historically been placed at a disadvantage and how those systems of inequity have fundamentally shaped the nature of our society, including our schools. According to Freire, education is never neutral; it either liberates or domesticates. When we lower expectations and devalue the lives of students of color, we are enacting a pedagogy of domestication.

ADDRESSING SYSTEMIC BARRIERS TO CULTURALLY AFFIRMING INSTRUCTION

It is not my intention to place blame on either teacher from the scenarios, or anyone else with similar practices. Society must reject unrealistic perceptions and expectations of teachers. A teacher is not good because she uses her own money to buy supplies, sacrifices her personal time and health for the good of her students, and neglects her family. A teacher is not bad because she is human and still learning. Society and popular culture have created caricatures of good teachers and bad teachers that we too often perpetuate when dealing with their real-life counterparts. Until we learn that teachers are simultaneously humans worthy of compassion and professionals worthy of respect, we will continue to do our educators injustice.

While I actively work to reject deficit perspectives of families, I also seek not to project deficits onto teachers. My coauthors and I started this work because the preservice teachers we served were only exhibiting a surface-level understanding of teaching for equity. Without examining their own identities and those of their students, as well as evaluating the curriculum and their own pedagogy, it is impossible for educators to internalize the processes and practices essential to culturally responsive instruction.

Too often, doing this work is considered "one more thing" on teachers' plates. Compiling text sets from the library and other resources requires time outside of the workday. With lives and families of their own, why should educators be expected to spend their personal time working? Why does this responsibility fall on the teacher alone? Why aren't these resources more readily available and embedded in the curricular materials provided by the school or district?

Over fifty percent of our student population is non-white. Why then are major booksellers, companies that produce hundreds of thousands of texts designed specifically for use in daily classroom instruction, profiting off of text sets that grossly misrepresent our population?

While some in publishing claim there are challenges to producing multicultural literature, they still acknowledge these decisions are market and profit driven. Why is the educational community still investing in such materials, rather than demanding better products? When selecting the materials for purchase, were teachers involved in the decision-making? Was the focus on the children in the classroom or on the "science of reading" sticker on the box? If there is to be change in the creation and selection of classroom materials, administrators and educators will have to become critical and informed consumers and will have to be recognized as competent professionals.

As we're learning from the science of reading conversations, most teachers need and want more professional learning (PL) opportunities on literacy instruction. Since it's not one more thing, such PL should be enacted through an equity lens. Unfortunately, this is often not what occurs. Too often, however, the "support and training [teachers] receive is episodic, myopic, and often meaningless" and further "the time and opportunities essential to intense, sustained professional development with regular follow-up and reinforcement are simply not in place in most contexts" (Darling-Hammond et al., 2009, pp. 2, 27). This may be due to the sizable financial investment required for the implementation of effective, continuous PL (Novak, 2018).

Nonetheless, research indicates investment in PL is worthwhile given the relationships between teacher quality and student learning outcomes and between teacher quality and PL (Archibald et al., 2011; Novak, 2018). Well-developed PL communities (PLCs) have a positive impact on both teaching practice and student achievement (Vescio et al., 2008; Zepeda, 2019). "PLCs offer an infrastructure to create the supportive cultures and conditions necessary for achieving significant gains . . . and for assisting teachers to become more effective in their work with students" (Morrissey, 2000, p. 3). Such PLCs reflect a new approach that moves away from the event-based, top-down professional development of the past. Impactful PL is embedded in teachers' contexts, continuous, and buoyed by the teachers' ability to witness student results firsthand (Guskey, 2002; Novak, 2018; Smagorinsky, 2018). Guskey (1997) found that teachers themselves related becoming "better teachers" to improved student outcomes, meaning the PL has to be contextualized and applied in teachers' classrooms.

Across the literature, descriptions of high-quality professional learning include common characteristics such as teacher collaboration and leadership, a focus on content and how students learn, connections to high standards, and extended duration and follow-up (Desimone et al., 2002). In other words, while moving toward more effective PL, researchers and PL facilitators must explicitly move away from prescriptive instruction to instruction that is more culturally responsive for teachers. Much like we advocate CRP for students, teacher learning needs to meet the needs of teachers and their specific contexts, beliefs, and challenges (Overstreet, 2017; Smagorinsky, 2018). CRP must be continuously and deeply embedded in learning at all levels (Ladson-Billings, 2000; Gay, 2018; Paris & Alim, 2017).

Even when educators have the knowledge and drive to teach in culturally responsive ways, they still don't always have the freedom to do so. As I mentioned at the beginning of this chapter, we are living through an era of censorship that is negatively impacting teachers and schools. Between book bannings, mandates against teaching about race, gender, and sexual orientation, and all the other restrictions on teachers, this work is both more difficult and more important than ever.

How can a single teacher combat so many systemic barriers? This is where the fifth component of our framework is so crucial. If we're going to enact social change, we must work collectively. There are complex and powerful systems in place that hinder educators' best efforts, forcing them to try doing all the deep, time-consuming work while also receiving all the blame for unsatisfactory student outcomes. Remember, beyond understanding ourselves, our students, our curriculum, and our pedagogy, we must consider how we can use this knowledge to enact change in our systems and communities—and invite students to do so as well.

PRACTICAL APPLICATION

Hopefully, this book will "help teachers shift the conversation away from what they think they can't do to what they could do . . . [and] move teachers from considering whether they can include particular lessons or particular texts in their instruction to how they might find multiple, even creative, ways to address the larger systems that enable homophobia and heterosexism" (Hermann-Wilmarth & Ryan, 2015, p. 436), as well as all the other "isms."

As an educator, you have likely faced many of these challenges. New challenges will undoubtedly arise throughout your career as you strive to do what's best for the students in your charge. Sometimes it will be scary or seem impossible. After all, you have to support yourself and we want to keep teachers like you in the classroom. So, how do you find the cracks in the barriers? How do you keep both your job and your conscience intact?

- **Study the laws and mandates.** Oftentimes, we react to restrictive laws and mandates by censoring ourselves. It is easy to overcorrect out of fear and frustration. Instead, carefully study the letter of the law. Where are there holes? Where are there exceptions? What is unclear? How can you leverage that information to find the cracks in the barrier and teach within them?
- **Know your standards.** As we discussed in our first book, standards can provide protection for culturally affirming and responsive teaching. Since these practices aren't "one more thing," they're embedded throughout your instruction and should be aligned with the standards you're beholden to. You're not just using diverse texts, for example, you're using high-quality, engaging texts to teach kids how to summarize, infer, identify the main idea, recognize rhyming words, identify root words and affixes, and so on. You should always keep the goal or target in mind and ensure you're meeting the standards of your subject area.
- **Be proactive and transparent.** Sometimes, preventative measures go a long way. If you're concerned about pushback against your instruction or materials, plan accordingly. Rather than waiting to be found out, let your classroom community know up front what your plans are. This might mean including upcoming units/topics and book lists in family newsletters or other communications. Explain the standards and other learning targets you're addressing and help families to feel like partners in their students' education. Remember that the most vocal people might not be the majority. There are many parents and caretakers who want their children to be better prepared to thrive in a diverse world. So, while you might have to have uncomfortable conversations and even modify instruction for some individuals, you might also find allies and opportunities.
- **Build community.** Remember that this isn't work that can or should be done alone. Find your co-conspirators. Who can you ideate and freedom dream with? Who can you go to for support? Who should you follow on social media, podcasts, and other outlets to help stay informed and find helpful resources? You are not alone, even though it may feel like it. If you're reading this book, you're already growing your community. We're with you.

- **Take care of yourself.** You can't pour from an empty cup. The longer I remain in education and equity work, the more I know this to be true. It can be absolutely exhausting trying to stand against the constant onslaught of bad news and worse practice. You will not have the capacity to take on every challenge. You won't have the energy to fight every day. You will feel discouraged and defeated sometimes. That's okay. Feel your feelings. Take breaks. Carve time and space for yourself away from your identity as teacher, advocate, and superhero. You're a human who deserves grace and space, to be whole and complex. You contain multitudes. Feed your outside passions. Move your body. Get outside in the sunshine. Rest, refuel, and refresh. Your students need you to be well.

STOP AND REFLECT

- What barriers are impeding your culturally responsive teaching goals?
- Where are the cracks in those barriers?
- Which rules or guidelines can you bend? Which rules cannot be broken?
- In what ways might you be self-censoring?
- Where in your curriculum is there space to incorporate students' interests, experiences, and knowledge?
- How might you supplement or replace elements of mandated lessons or materials?
- Who are your co-conspirators with whom you can brainstorm small acts of resistance?
- What resources and online communities might be useful to you as you do this work?
- How are you communicating your goals, learning targets, and standard alignment with families? How might you proactively engage families in their students' learning?
- How are you intentionally creating space for yourself to rest?

Chapter 2

Using Texts to Explore Identity, Community, Storytelling, and Standards

SCENARIO

Mrs. Patil teaches sixth grade at a large, urban middle school. While teachers at her school are given pacing guides with themes and standards for instruction, they have autonomy to select the texts and materials that reach those expectations. This month, sixth graders are studying "identity" using the following standard:

- W.6.3: Write narratives to develop real or imagined experiences or events using effective technique, relevant descriptive details, and well-structured event sequences.
  - d. Use precise words and phrases, relevant descriptive details, and sensory language to convey experiences and events.

To teach this standard, Mrs. Patil decides to use the short story "Eleven" by Sandra Cisneros as a mentor text. She begins the lesson by reading the story aloud to students as they follow along in their textbook. She points out a few examples of similes and metaphors throughout the story as she reads. At the conclusion of the story, she tells students they will be writing a personal narrative about their eleventh birthday. She tells them to begin brainstorming by making a list of everything they did for their eleventh birthday. They are then instructed to use their list to write their narrative.

Writing often takes a backseat in literacy and language arts classrooms. We recognize this is often due to time constraints and testing obligations (which often fail to include writing). As educators, we believe writing to be a robust process that includes multiple resources for students to read, view, listen to, etc. prior to the writing process. We also believe that writing using the narrative writing standard allows us to tap into multiple components of our framework, including: 1. *Learning about our students* (Who are students? What funds of knowledge do they bring to the classroom?); 2. *Evaluating the curriculum* (Which materials will we use?); 3. *Reflecting on pedagogy* (How will we teach in a way that engages students and validates and affirms their voices and experiences?); 4. *Social change* (How can we ask our students to consider how they may take action toward social change based on their new learning?).

FRAMEWORK CONNECTIONS

Mrs. Patil's unit theme is identity, so it connects nicely to the narrative writing standard she chose, and it also connects to the first part of our framework, which speaks to *learning about the lives, identities, and experiences of students*. This might look different across different grade levels, but by middle school, we definitely want students to take a deep dive into exploring their identities. This means extending beyond, "Tell me about a time when. . . . " Identity work should help students connect to their culture, community, history, and personal experiences. Narrative writing is a place where students can explore these topics.

In considering the *curriculum* piece of our framework, as literacy educators, one of the greatest challenges we face is choosing texts to use in our classrooms, particularly when thinking about our obligations to meet required state or national standards. In addition, we have to consider how to engage our students in culturally responsive instruction while also facing the increasing challenge of banned books. Often, teachers choose a diverse text, just as Mrs. Patil has, but we believe providing multiple texts for students to explore can be beneficial. When exploring multiple texts, we should include texts from a range of genres, representing a variety of formats including poems, speeches, song lyrics, podcasts, articles, websites, videos, and images. This variety of texts also offers different levels of text complexity for students, providing opportunities for scaffolding, if needed. When students engage with multiple texts, they are required to think more critically, and they gain in-depth knowledge of content from multiple perspectives. This can also provide them with the opportunity to explore different writing styles, authors' craft, vocabulary, and text structures. In addition, students can engage in comparative reading, analyzing topics across texts instead of engaging in isolated reading of one text or perspective.

This approach provides opportunities for students to hear new ideas, new voices, and to step into the lives and experiences of others through stories, music, or images. Access to multiple texts allows us to think critically and question what we know or perhaps what we think we know about a particular topic based on information that we have been provided in one singular text. Even with a theme like identity, hearing multiple perspectives can spark reflections and new thinking about our own experiences and how we have navigated and continue to navigate those experiences. Inviting students into the worlds of others as they explore their own can help them connect to the reading and writing process.

Dr. Muhammed (2020) tells us that students are sometimes disconnected from texts both in and out of schools for a number of reasons. She cites the lack of diversity and representation of authorship and thought and the lack of multimodal content paired with traditional print text. She asserts that readings chosen for the classroom are not always responsive to student identities, histories, and literacies, and she shares that teachers don't always find connections to students' lives through texts. With this knowledge in mind, we will seek to help students connect to the learning process by providing access to multiple, diverse texts that address these issues and get our students more connected and motivated to read. When choosing texts, it is important to explore content that will help to share students' understanding of themselves, others, and the world around them. We ask, what texts can we share that will provide "mirrors and windows" (Bishop, 1990) into the lived experiences of others to help them reflect on their own experiences, and to help them understand the world?

Our framework goes beyond curriculum materials as we extensively *focus on pedagogy* and our commitment to teach in a way that engages students and validates and affirms their voices and experiences. One way we focus on pedagogy is to ensure we make space for students to engage in dialogue with each other as they navigate the learning process. We also believe in teaching through an integrated approach that includes both reading and writing. This provides an opportunity for students to consume, critique, analyze, explore, and reflect on new information and knowledge they are obtaining. Mrs. Patil integrates reading and writing, but it is our hope to engage in this process more thoroughly, providing extensive opportunities for students to write in response to their reading, and using writing as an opportunity to not only reflect on the text they are reading, but to turn their lens to the writing standards and engage in mini low-stakes writing pieces that can potentially be expanded into full-assessment written pieces as desired. This might include daily writing prompts or quick writes where students engage in writing that connects them to texts, writing that helps them question the text or the world, or writing that helps them engage their imaginations in new adventures.

These small pieces can be a part of their writing journals, where they revisit and revise them over time, potentially creating a more formal writing piece of their choice. This approach provides students with opportunities to explore many topics, share their voices, and *choose* a piece to fully develop as a final standards-aligned product.

When considering *how* we teach related to topics such as identity, we begin the planning process understanding there are state and district mandates, while also asking ourselves how we can help our students meet academic goals while critically exploring the world and their identities. We seek to include student interests through reading and writing (literacy) to share the stories they are learning and the stories they are living. Throughout this chapter, we provide examples of using reading and writing to validate and affirm the identities and experiences of students, while meeting required standards and embedding our framework in the process.

In embracing opportunities for writing in our lessons, we also see this as an opportunity for students to consider and reflect upon how they can enact *change* in their communities, classrooms, and the world. What are areas that need improvement? What is our potential role in that improvement? We always want students to focus on the joy and cultural wealth surrounding their identities and communities. We also hope they will continue to reflect on how to view the world through a critical lens that we can always continue to impact through positive change. Literature can be a tool in this process.

DISRUPTING THE SCENARIO

In the previous scenario, Mrs. Patil has chosen a mentor text from the student textbook to share with students. To begin the lesson, she jumps right into reading the short story, without providing any background knowledge or allowing the students to make connections to the text topic. This is a story about an experience the main character has on her birthday at school. Mrs. Patil could have started the lesson by asking students to reflect on memorable experiences they have had in school, either positive, negative, or neutral. She could ask them how the experience impacted them, what they learned or gained from it, and how it helps them to understand who they are in school or out of school and how they engage with others. Tricia Ebarvia reminds us of the importance of helping students get "proximate to others' stories . . . so we can help students step into conversations responsibly about how we treat others and who we are as a society" (2023, p. 91). Posing these questions as a pre-reading activity could help students in this process as they prepare to read an important story about a young girl who wasn't treated well by others. Literature has the power to help us consider the ways in which we show up for others in the world. Simply reading a story with no discussion or opportunity to reflect or get "proximate" is not aligned with culturally responsive instruction.

As she reads the text aloud, Mrs. Patil only focuses on pointing out similes and metaphors, not considering other language that might evoke sensory images for students as required by the standard. Mrs. Patil could have also focused on language that evoked emotions like when the main character describes how her years are pushing at the back of her eyes and her face is hot and she's making animal noises. This language in context is powerful. She could have also asked questions that helped students make personal connections to the text, language that helped them understand the identities of the characters, and how their own identities might be similar or different. Mrs. Patil could have asked students to consider how they may have felt if they were put in this situation.

By simply reading the story, Mrs. Patil does not provide any opportunities for students to practice engaging with the text individually through activities like double journal entries or writing breaks. She also fails to provide opportunities for students to work collaboratively with their peers in activities like "two-minute talks" or "think/pair/shares." Providing stopping points along the way, where students could share their reactions to the text and showcase their learning, personal connections and comprehension could strengthen this lesson from a culturally responsive and standards-based perspective. For example, she could ask students questions from the first few paragraphs like, what do you think it means to feel six or five? What might this look like? What might make a kid want to sit in their mama's lap? What does it mean to feel "smart eleven" or "smart" any age? Tell your neighbor about a time when you wanted to say something to an adult, but you didn't quite know how to say it. These questions are asking students to share their cultural knowledge, prior experiences, and frames of references (Gay, 2010). These questions are responsive to students' ideas and experiences and can serve to make reading this text more relevant for them.

In addition, Mrs. Patil's attempt at modeling does not provide opportunities to consider the experiences of the narrator, the author's choices, or the experiences of students—all of which will be helpful as they begin writing their own narratives later. She could have also posed questions to the students, such as:

- How is the narrator feeling?
- What words does the author use to show this?
- How would you feel if this happened to you?
- What details does the author give that provide imagery?

- What do we learn about the main character's culture and identity through this story?

Mrs. Patil's approach does not provide opportunities for students to share their thinking around the reading or writing process. In addition, Mrs. Patil's lesson does not reflect the framework we developed for our teaching practices to integrate culturally responsive instruction. While she has used a text by Sandra Cisneros, we would encourage her to use several texts representing diverse perspectives of youth narrators discussing diverse topics. In addition, we would encourage Mrs. Patil to offer choice to students. Perhaps students simply do not want to write about their eleventh birthday. This lack of choice also fails to take into account that students might not celebrate birthdays at all due to cultural or religious reasons. Teaching narrative writing is an opportunity for us to ask students, *what stories do you want to share about yourself? About the people and places that shape your identity? What stories do you want to share about your community? Your friends, your hopes? Dreams?*

While Mrs. Patil's lesson uses an engaging text and provides a prompt that is specific to student identity and experience, we want to provide opportunities that go beyond these traditional approaches and provide a myriad of ways for students to engage in culturally responsive texts and prepare for authentic narrative writing experiences. In the following lesson, with the same standard in mind—"*W.6.3: Write narratives to develop real or imagined experiences or events using effective technique, relevant descriptive details, and well-structured event sequences, D. Use precise words and phrases, relevant descriptive details, and sensory language to convey experiences and events.*" We want to extend the lesson theme beyond identity to include, "Identity, community and storytelling." Through this lesson we hope to provide a more culturally responsive approach to this standard. By adjusting the theme, we are able to bring together components that are important to the learning process for students, especially when we consider tapping into their interests and experiences and connecting to standards. By adding community, we are able to explore the places within the stories we will read and consider the community history and assets there. We can also consider this as we ask students to write their own stories. We want them to explore their community assets and histories as well. This is incredibly important because so often students share, "I don't have any community assets" or "There is nothing special about my culture." We have to speak back to this mindset and help students learn and share their counterstories. We can help students see community and cultural assets by asking about important places in their communities, the languages or special sayings in their family, the history of their communities, special occasions and traditions. Sharing our own community and cultural asset stories can be helpful as well. This approach gives students an opportunity to disrupt this mindset and instead think about how our communities can be a place of knowledge, comfort, and resources.

Finally, by adding "storytelling," we are teaching students that narrative writing can be a form of storytelling. Through this lens, we can meet the standards as well.

PRACTICAL APPLICATION

We often hear that teachers don't have time to explore students' identities and meet the standards, and as we state in our last book, it's not "one more thing." We can do it all. We can engage in exploring identities, communities, storytelling, and meeting the standards all at the same time. It is the integrated approach to how we engage in the teaching and learning process. It is also how we make space for student voices and gifts in our classrooms. Dr. Muhammad tells us, "If we do not center their gifts, we should not be the ones to teach them. For so long, children have had their stories told from deficit perspectives" (2023, p. 15). Through this integrated approach, we provide space for children to tell their own stories.

I (Christy) have modeled this lesson with preservice and inservice teachers. To begin, I draw on Dr. Muhammad's approach to teaching and understanding identity with her prompt about important places "If you could take me somewhere to help me understand your culture, where would you take me" (Muhammad, 2020, p. 72). To this prompt, I add the questions, *Why? What would you want me to learn? What would I notice? What might I wonder?* This short prompt from Muhammad has proven to be incredibly powerful. First, it brings us together and allows us to center ourselves (I do the activity with them), while focusing on identity, culture, community, and storytelling. Next, it provides an opportunity for students to share themselves with us in ways that are important to them. Through this activity, my students have taken me to their family farms, to the markets where they sell the food from their farm. They have taken me to Nigeria, to India, to their favorite vacation spot, to their backyards, to their grandmother's homes. This opening activity lays the foundation for identity work and storytelling.

Next, as I introduce the standard we will be using, which is focused on writing narratives, I want to explore several texts with students. So, as previously mentioned, having a range of texts is important as we focus on narrative writing that centers identity and community. Access to a diverse range of texts will allow students to explore the identities of others while also exploring the cultural wealth and community assets across diverse communities. This approach will also provide an opportunity for students to connect to their identities and explore the role of storytelling.

Here, I will share some titles that focus on storytelling, community, and identity. I have used these readings to explore the author's craft, and as a springboard for writing. Specifically, I have asked students to use these mentor texts to consider how an author writes, according to the standards, but I have also asked them in this process, as I suggested in the reflection on Mrs. Patil's lesson, to consider their own communities, their own identities, and to engage in the art of storytelling to share their experiences. In providing opportunities for students to read a range of texts, we also want them to have opportunities to engage in mini writing responses that provide space for them to make connections, reflect on their learning, and reflect on their own experiences based on these texts. These varied opportunities can give students a chance to share and reflect on their responses to determine if this mini writing idea is a topic they would like to develop further for an expanded narrative writing piece. In table 2.1, I have provided several examples of texts that could be used to focus on storytelling, community, and identity across grades K–12. It also includes example writing prompts that ask students to explore these concepts as well. In the case of longer texts, I have used excerpts with students. In addition to these traditional texts, I also include a range of poems, song lyrics, and visual images as options for giving students access to diverse texts on the same topic.

As a reminder, these writing prompts would occur as students view these texts through the lens of a mentor text exploring components of literacy standards, including how authors might engage the reader, use figurative language, setting, and character development. You could also determine other literacy standards you would like to address with these texts. However, these writing prompts allow students to go beyond the author's purpose and craft to the writing stage where they begin to share about themselves, the places that shape their identities, their communities, and the art of storytelling through multiple processes. These writing prompts are here to show you how to use meaningful, diverse texts to provide mini opportunities for students to engage in narrative writing, sharing, and reflection activities around similar topics, across multiple grade levels. You may be wondering, "What could this look like in a classroom if I wanted to choose an anchor text, focus on identity, community, and storytelling while meeting the standards?" Here's an example.

TEXTS

For this example, I am choosing *Some Places More Than Others* as my anchor text. So, after using the introduction activity from Muhammad (2020) "Take me to a place. . . . " I would introduce this text to students. I chose this

Table 2.1 Several examples of texts that could be used to focus on storytelling, community, and identity across grades K–12

Text title	Summary	Mini writing prompts that explore identity, community, and storytelling
My Papi Has a Motorcycle by Isabel Quintero	*My Papi Has a Motorcycle* by Isabel Quintero is a **picture book** about a little girl who goes on a motorcycle ride with her papi when he comes home. They travel through the city and talk about all of the amazing places in the community.	**Example 1:** Read the story, *My Papi Has a Motorcycle* by Isabel Quintero. After reading the story, revisit this quote, and allow students to write. "There's the school where we practice soccer! There's the post office where Mr. Charlie takes our letters! And la panaderia where Papi buys conchas on Sunday mornings." **Prompts for students:** What are some important places in your community? Why are these places important to you? What do you like to do there? Why are these places important to your community? Be sure to include specific details about your place in your response. Revisit the author's use of details in this story. How did these details help you visualize the places important to the narrator? How can details help your reader visualize the important places in your community? Allow time for students to share their responses with a partner or in small groups, sharing their experiences and pride in their communities. **Example 2:** Read the story, *My Papi Has a Motorcycle* by Isabel Quintero. After reading the story, revisit this quote, and allow students to write. "No matter how far I go from this place, or how much it changes, this city will always be with me." **Prompt for students:** What parts of your current or previous community will always be with you? Why? Be sure to use descriptive details and sensory language to help the reader understand your experiences connected to your community. *This prompt might really speak to students who have lived in different places. Here they get to explore how our communities are always a part of our history and identity and share this with others.

Text title	Summary	Mini writing prompts that explore identity, community, and storytelling
Alma and How She Got Her Name by Juana Martinez-Neal	Alma and How She Got Her Name by Juana Martinez-Neal is a **picture book** about a young girl who thinks she has too many names. In a discussion with her father about her names she learns about the important history and culture of people in her family.	**Example 3:** Read the story, Alma and How She Got Her Name by Juana Martinez-Neal. **Prompts for students:** In the story, Alma's father tells her about her relatives, their characteristics, their talents, things they enjoyed, etc. At the end, the author tells us the story of her name and then asks, "What story would you like to tell?" Ask students to write the story they would like to tell about themselves. Do they want to write about their name? The things that make them special? Their talents? Things they enjoy? Do they want to write this in the form of a story, a poem, or an art piece? Give them options for sharing their identity. Encourage them to use figurative language, descriptive details, and accurate event sequences. Guide them in brainstorming and organizing their ideas.
Some Places More Than Others by Renée Watson	Some Places More Than Others by Renée Watson is a **middle grade novel** about a young girl whose father is from New York, but she has never been to New York. There are some tensions between her father and her grandfather who lives in New York. The main character, Amara, finally convinces her family to allow her to make the journey to New York with her father. She learns so much about her cultural history.	**Example 4:** Read the excerpt from Some Places More Than Others by Renée Watson when the narrator Amara asks her grandfather, "What does your heart carry with you? What memories do you hold?" (p. 131). **Prompts for students:** What does your heart carry? Joy? Peace? Worry? Sadness? Love? What memories do you hold? What important places are a part of your memory? What important places contribute to your joy, peace, and love? ――――――――― **Example 5:** Read the excerpt from Some Places More Than Others by Renée Watson. "We turn right on Third Street, and then we walk to a building that has a mural painted on it. One half is of a man's face. His eyes look heavy, like they are holding worry and pain but also passion. 'This is Reverend Pedro Pietri. He was a Puerto Rican civil rights activist. . . . This place is legendary for playwrights, poets, and musicians of color whose work isn't always accepted by the mainstream industry'" (p. 158).

| | | **Prompts for students:** Tell us about an authentic place in your community that holds history and speaks to the talents and assets your community has to offer. Try to choose a place that you would enjoy learning more about as you engage in this task. Write a story about this place. Be sure to include specific details and events. You can revisit Amara's journey in New York and how the author shows us the historical places in her community there. How does the author introduce these places? What techniques and details are used? Consider these examples as you write about the historical place in your community.
*This could be a narrative writing piece or an informational writing piece.

Example 6: In *Some Places More than Others*, the narrator Amara found amazing places to tell us a story of New York and how it connected to her own culture.
Prompts for students: Create a multimedia project that shows the amazing places in your city or in a city in which you've lived or a city that is important to your family history and/or culture. How is this city connected to your identity? Your culture? Why is this city important to you? This project can include images, interviews, poetry (your original poetry or poetry by others), at least one informational text, music, maps, etc. Tell us an amazing story through multiple perspectives.

Example 7: Read the excerpt from *Indian No More*. "Then the elder wailed. . . . The other men joined in, repeating this and singing a song I'd never heard. I leaned over to Chich, my curiosity piqued. 'What are they singing?' I whispered. 'It's an honor song, sweetie, for your chup,' Chich said. 'How do they all know the song?' 'They heard it many times before. It's been passed down from family to family" (p. 10).
Prompt for students: What songs, traditions, artifacts, ideas, ceremonies, etc. have been passed down in your community?
*This prompt also provides an opportunity for students to engage in community research by interviewing the elders in their community, interviewing people in their family, and asking them about traditions, ceremonies, etc. This prompt is a great opportunity for students to hear stories and tell stories. |
|---|---|---|
| *Indian No More* by Charlene Willing Mcmanis and Traci Sorell | *Indian No More* by Charlene Willing Mcmanis and Traci Sorell is a **middle grade novel** about a young girl who has to reconsider her identity as she is forced to move from the Grand Ronde reservation to Los Angeles. She comes to learn more about her own culture and the culture of others as she explores the importance of community, identity, and history. | |

Text title	Summary	Mini writing prompts that explore identity, community, and storytelling
Clap When You Land by Elizabeth Acevedo	*Clap When You Land* by Elizabeth Acevedo is a **young adult novel** told in verse about two young girls. One of them lives in New York and one of them lives in the Dominican Republic. Their worlds collide as a tragedy that impacts both of them changes their lives forever. The role of community and identity is so rich in Acevedo's storytelling.	**Example 8:** Read the excerpt from *Clap When You Land* by Elizabeth Acevedo. "Mami wanted me to be a lady: sit up straight, cross my ankles, let men protect me. Papi wanted me to be a leader. To think quick & strike hard, to speak rarely, but when I did, to always be heard. Me? Playing chess taught me a queen is both: deadly & graceful, poised & ruthless. Quiet & cunning. A queen." **Prompts to students:** Who do people in your life want you to be? Your teachers? Your friends? Your family members? Strangers? What do they tell you about who you should be? Who do they say you are? Who do you say you are?
"Ode to Family Photographs" by Gary Soto	"Ode to Family Photographs" is a poem about reflecting on family experiences and memories.	**Example 9:** Read the poem "Ode to Family Photographs" by Gary Soto. In this poem, he discusses the photographs taken by his mother. **Prompts to students:** Choose two or three family or friend photographs that are important to you (and that you would like to share). Write a brief story about the photographs. Why are these photographs important to you? Who are in the pictures? Where were the pictures taken? How do these photographs represent your identity, culture, connections to places, and/or family? As you write your story about the photographs, be sure the events in your story are well-structured. What happened first? Who are the characters/people in your story? What is the setting? You can revisit the stories you have read in this lesson and examine how the authors sequence the events in their stories. Will this work for your photograph stories?

Table 2.2 List of texts used to accompany the anchor text

Poems:	• "The Negro Speaks of Rivers" by Langston Hughes • "Harlem" by Langston Hughes • "The New Colossus" by Emma Lazarus
Visual Images:	• Photos of Harriet Tubman Memorial in New York. Choose from images from the Smithsonian American Art Museum • African American art: Harlem Renaissance, civil rights era, and beyond selection for images from the Harlem Renaissance
Informational Text:	• A New African American Identity: The Harlem Renaissance from the National Museum of African American History & Culture • The history of Times Square
Music:	• *Drop Me Off in Harlem* by Ella Fitzgerald featuring Duke Ellington • *Welcome to New York* by Taylor Swift • *Manhattan* by Ella Fitzgerald

text because of the focus on community, storytelling, and identity as Amara tries to learn more about her family and culture. She tries to learn more about New York, which is where her father is from, so there are so many connections to community and place. It is also a beautiful representation of how our communities are intrinsically linked to our identities.

I begin with standards. As mentioned in chapter 1, this is one way to address mandates and navigate barriers. We know we must address them, so I have a reading standard, *RL.6.9: Compare and contrast texts in different forms or genres (e.g., stories and poems; historical novels and fantasy stories) in terms of their approaches to similar themes and topics* and a writing standard, *W.6.3: Write narratives to develop real or imagined experiences or events using effective technique, relevant descriptive details, and well-structured event sequences.* My goal is for students to read the anchor text and other texts, exploring the cultures of others and the experiences and identities of others, then turn that lens to themselves and explore their identities and experiences as well.

In connection to our discussion earlier about choosing texts, see table 2.2 for a list of texts used to accompany the anchor text.

You will notice I have chosen some poems, visual images from The Smithsonian American Art Museum website and from the African American art selection as well. I have included informational text from the National Museum of African American History and Culture and then a blog on the history of Times Square. I included music as well because students are often motivated by it. You will see "Drop Me Off in Harlem" by Fitzgerald & Ellington and "Welcome to New York" by Taylor Swift. I intentionally chose these texts because we are addressing the comparing and contrasting standard. I want to explore these two songs with students and think about perspectives. There are several resources in this table and it is not likely you would have time to use all of them in a lesson, but I did want to provide several of them for you here and would encourage you to add more based on the needs, identities, and experiences of your students. You can also ask for input from students in choosing resources. They could choose some of their favorite songs, poems, or images as well. Giving students choice and tapping into their culture and interests aligns with our framework of culturally responsive teaching.

EXPLORING IDENTITY, COMMUNITY, STORYTELLING AND STANDARDS, OH MY!

Table 2.3 shows several writing opportunities for students for this unit. These opportunities include exploration of multiple texts from table 2.2, as well as exploration of identity, community, and storytelling *while* meeting the standards.

In these tasks, you will notice students are being given the opportunity to compare texts, sometimes in the same genre and sometimes across genres as described in the standard. For example, in the music example, students are asked to compare two songs. They are comparing two songs that are in different genres of music but they are still songs, so they are then asked to compare these to a text as well. While students are given the opportunity to share their learning through storytelling in some of the tasks, the task 5 example is an explicit link to storytelling. This task connects to students' identities and gives them some choice in what they would like to include. In addition, we are addressing the writing narrative standard. Again, it's not likely that you would use all of the texts or tasks provided, but choosing what might work for you and your students and adding and deleting options can yield the same results. Considering a variety of texts that work for your students will help them find success in meeting the standards, and challenge them appropriately. Also, consider which ones they will find connections to and be motivated to read/view/hear.

These texts and experiences align with our framework in that they encourage us to consider identities and curriculum. They provide content that values and affirms the lived experiences and communities of students, which can serve to teach others to appreciate these experiences and potentially limit the harm based on the ignorance of others.

As mentioned at the beginning of this chapter, we also want to encourage students to engage in and consider social change. The following examples are options that allow for students to consider how they might be able to engage in social change based on their learning and learning experiences with these texts. In this unit, students have read extensively about beautiful, diverse

Table 2.3 Several writing opportunities for students

Identity, community, and storytelling	Task	Standard
Identity	Task 1: On pages 160–61, Amara's father tells her all of the ways she's like people in her family. What characteristics do you share with others in your family? You may have to interview family members to learn more about them and the connections you may have. Write a poem, short story, song, or journal entry to show what you've learned about your connections to others. Make it creative!	W.6.3: Write narratives to develop real or imagined experiences or events using effective technique, relevant descriptive details, and well-structured event sequences.
Identity, Storytelling	Task 2: On page 172, Amara's dad shares his poem inspired by Langston Hughes's "Mother to Son." Read Hughes's poem and compare and contrast Hughes's poem and Amara's father's poem. How are they similar? How are they different? Write a poem about someone special in your life. Why are they special? What impact have they had on your life? Share this through your poetry!	W.6.3: Write narratives to develop real or imagined experiences or events using effective technique, relevant descriptive details, and well-structured event sequences.
Community, Identity	Task 3: Listen to "Drop Me Off in Harlem" by Fitzgerald & Ellington and "Welcome to New York" by Taylor Swift. Read the lyrics as you listen. Listen multiple times if needed. These songs are both about New York, but how are they different? How might the artists' identities contribute to these differences? How might the time period in which they are written contribute to these differences? Why might their perspectives be different? How are they similar? How are these songs similar and different to Amara's experience as described in Some Places? Find a song that represents your city or town. Is this song an accurate depiction? Why or why not?	RL.6.9: Compare and contrast texts in different forms or genres (e.g., stories and poems; historical novels and fantasy stories) in terms of their approaches to similar themes and topics.

Identity, community, and storytelling	Task	Standard
Community	Task 4: On pages 101–02, Amara describes the Harriet Tubman memorial. Write a summary of what she says, then draw your version of the memorial. Finally, view an image of the memorial (link above). How does Amara's description compare to the visual image? How are they similar, how are they different? Which did you prefer and why? What does each writer/creator do to engage you in this piece? Find an important place that is representative of your community and the history of your community. Research this place and be prepared to share with us what you've learned! Write a description of this place and include a picture. How is this place connected to your community?	RL.6.9: Compare and contrast texts in different forms or genres (e.g., stories and poems; historical novels and fantasy stories) in terms of their approaches to similar themes and topics *You could also add a research standard here.
Community, Identity, Storytelling	Task 5: Amara found amazing places to tell us a story of New York and how it connected to her own culture. Create a multimedia project that shows the amazing places in your city or in a city in which you've lived or a city that is important to your family history and/or culture. How is this city connected to your identity? Your culture? Why is this city important to you? This project can include images, interviews, poetry (your original poetry or poetry by others), at least one informational text, music, maps, etc. Tell us an amazing story through multiple perspectives.	W.6.3: Write narratives to develop real or imagined experiences or events using effective technique, relevant descriptive details, and well-structured event sequences. *You could also add a technology standard here.

Table 2.4 Conclusion to the unit on exploring identity, community, and storytelling

SOCIAL CHANGE

Example 1: Throughout the texts you have explored identity, community, and storytelling. Reflect on how the authors reveal **identities** in texts. Revisit the texts if needed. For example, how do we learn about Amara's identity? How do we learn about the character's identity in Hughes's "Mother to Son"? How were the identities you read about similar to your own identity? How were they different? As a school, a country, a society, how can we show that we value all identities? Can you think of examples in the real world where all identities aren't valued? What can you personally do to value all identities?

Example 2: In this example, you can simply replace identity with community. Throughout the texts you have explored identity, community, and storytelling. Reflect on how the authors reveal **communities** in texts. Revisit the texts if needed. For example, how do we learn about Amara's community in New York? How were the communities you read about similar to your own community? How were they different? How can we show that we value all communities? Can you think of examples in the real world where all communities aren't valued? What can you personally do to value all communities?

Example 3: As you read about communities in this unit, you read about how people value their communities and the important people and places in diverse communities. We have seen the beauty and resources in communities through libraries, murals, soccer fields, community stores, etc. You have also had several opportunities to share and reflect on the beauty of your own community. We want to continue to protect our communities and the histories and experiences they hold. What are different ways you can support your community? Use reliable, recent, relevant sources from the internet to research ways to help your community. Choose one thing you would like to do to support people, events, or organizations in your community. Create a plan that you could share with others to address this need.

identities and communities. They have had an opportunity to explore their own identities and communities as well. The reflection/conclusion piece of this project can provide an opportunity for students to think about how they can engage in action around these topics. The examples in table 2.4 can serve as a conclusion to the unit on exploring identity, community, and storytelling.

These examples are just a few ways to help students begin thinking about change in their communities and the broader world. We would invite you to seek their input on ideas as well.

CONCLUSION

While this unit is focused on identity, community, and storytelling, the major components could be connected to almost any unit. Remember, our guiding principles tell us that our teaching is not just about activities. Our teaching is a mindset that reflects what we believe about culturally responsive instruction, what we believe about how we hope students can bring their whole selves to their learning experiences in our classrooms, and how we hope students feel confident in how they navigate the world around them. This unit is just one example of that, and in this example, we focused on several pieces of our framework.

We focused on *learning about students*. This was accomplished by the opening identity activity, throughout the writing prompts, and with the closing activity. We also *evaluated and reflected on curriculum and pedagogy*. We were intentional about the texts we chose and how we wanted students to experience the text in a way that would help them not only address the standards, but also consider their own experiences, identities, and communities, engaging them in meaningful ways in the content. For so long, the majority of classroom stories have been told by and about white people. The texts we chose embraced diverse perspectives and were counternarratives to the stereotypical stories told about people of color. These texts were chosen with the hope of healing the generational harm of instructional choices that told dangerous half-truths about communities and people of color. They were chosen to counter those half-truths and highlight the beauty and brilliance of people and places who have traditionally been marginalized.

Additionally, this unit asked students to engage in *social change* efforts, to take their learning and consider how they can improve their communities. This framework is how we engage in culturally responsive instruction that benefits students in several ways. Through this unit, we provided an opportunity for students to engage in connecting to the cultures of others through their reading as well as their own cultures through reflection and writing. We also provided space for students to engage in the standards while not being asked to leave their experiences and identities behind in the process. Units like this can help students master standards while also encouraging a sense of belonging by affirming who students are, where they come from, and the stories they wish to share with the world. Through the act of storytelling, we believe dreaming and healing can occur. We believe harm has less space to breathe if we smother it with the validation, love, and beauty of our stories. Our students should be empowered to share their lives, learn about their culture and communities, and consider how they can positively impact the world through culturally responsive instruction.

Finally, in a chapter that focuses on identity, storytelling, and choosing texts, I want to make it clear that I understand the political contexts of our classrooms today related to identity and texts. A question that has often been posed to me is, "How can I select texts that embrace these ideas *and* are supported by parents and administrators?" This is a difficult question to answer because I recognize that all contexts are different, but I offer some suggestions:

- *Connect your text selections to the standards you are required to teach.* It is required that we teach standards, so how do the texts and topics we want to teach embrace this requirement?
- *Research and build a rationale around your instructional decisions* (Ryan & Hermann-Wilmarth, 2018). In other words, make sure you have research to support your instructional decisions. Look to the work of authors we have cited in this book like Rudine Sims Bishop, Gholdy Muhammad, Geneva Gay, Caitlin Ryan, Jill Hermann-Wilmarth, and Gloria Ladson-Billings. Research supports culturally responsive instruction!
- *Know your laws and policies* (Ryan & Hermann-Wilmarth, 2018). Know your laws and policies and consider how you can be an agent of change and how school and district leaders can support you in this work.
- *Know your sources of support, such as principals, librarians, and parents* (Ryan & Hermann-Wilmarth, 2018). Who else is doing this work in your school/district? How can you work together to create more sources of support?
- *Invite families into the conversation.* Families want to be a part of their child's education. As a parent, I was always interested in what my child was learning. This knowledge could help me navigate conversations at home about her learning. As a teacher, you can share with parents your teaching philosophy, the rationale for teaching what you teach (include research) and texts and activities you will use in your classroom, along with the standards. If you anticipate pushback, discuss with your principal and media specialists/librarians ahead of time and ask for guidance. Parents and administrators can be amazing partners in this work. Building relationships with them can help us better serve our students.
- *Let everyone know you value the humanity of all students and that your classroom is a place where we learn and share our ideas without harming or oppressing others.* Look for literature to use with students that authentically showcases these values.

We recognize there is a level of comfort you must have in doing this work and if you haven't reached that level of comfort, we encourage you to continue to learn, continue to study the history of our country, education systems, and the culture of your students. Every one of our students deserves a culturally responsive educator leading their classroom. Even if you have reached that level of comfort, we know there may still be times when we are faced with discomfort. Continue to learn and grow through that discomfort. Work in community and learn with others. We are all learning every day.

As we learn, grow, and navigate different levels of comfort, we can sometimes feel it is easier to retreat to the path of least resistance and planning. A dear friend recently shared with me her observations of classrooms in this political context where inservice and preservice teachers are finding it easier to retreat to books about crayons and animals instead of finding and utilizing texts that embrace culturally responsive pedagogy. When she shared this with me, I was reminded of José Vilson's words during the summer of 2023 when I attended the Reimagining Education Summer Institute. At that conference, Vilson powerfully shared, "Fear is often used as a tool to make people act against their own hearts." People acting against their own hearts can lead to self-censorship. It can lead to an abundance of books about crayons and bears in classrooms while erasing books about the beauty, joy, genius, experiences, and identities of marginalized communities. We should continue to examine our fears as well as our hearts, specifically how our responses to fear might betray our hearts and the needs of our students. For the sake of our students, let us not retreat.

STOP AND REFLECT

- As you choose texts, what knowledge do you want students to gain from these texts? How does this connect to content area standards? What knowledge do we want students to gain beyond the standards?
- How do tasks connect to students' culture and identity?
- How are students' cultures and identities being validated and affirmed in your classroom?
- How are students being asked to connect to the texts? How do they have opportunities to connect texts to their identities and experiences?
- How can you use reading and writing to engage students in community research?
- How can we explore identity, community, and storytelling through other disciplines, such as art, music, or dance?
- How can we encourage students to engage in text sets through social action?

Chapter 3

Making Space for Culturally Affirming and Responsive Literacy Assessment

SCENARIO

Mr. Higgins teaches third grade at a rural elementary school. This is his third year at the school. He stayed on after he completed his student teaching there. Mr. Higgins enjoys teaching at the school because many of his students are growing up in a similar rural environment as his upbringing. He feels that he already has a connection to his students because of this. Mr. Higgins also is diligent in bringing what he learned as a student teacher into his practices as a teacher, which includes the literacy assessments he is required to administer.

He knows that foundational reading skills are essential to student success, especially at this crucial third grade year, so he works to apply all he's learned from recent trainings on the science of reading. Because he knows assessment should drive instruction, Mr. Higgins assesses students' reading skills early and often. In addition to giving the required DIBELS assessments that test his students' awareness of letter-sound correspondence and oral reading passages to test their reading levels, he is careful to check for reading comprehension skills by having them read passages and answer multiple choice comprehension questions. He is not surprised to discover most of his students are reading well below grade level and will require intensive instruction in reading foundational skills.

Assessment is a part of daily life for educators. We are constantly checking in with our students about what they know, what they want to know, and how they are learning new information. In our conversations with practicing educators, we often hear stories of assessments that are mandated by local school districts with little room for agency. We also know that sometimes (okay, maybe often) "assessment" is lumped together with words like "tests" and "required" or phrases like "data driven" and "state mandated." For many educators the word "assessment" conjures up feelings of dread, obligation, concern, frustration, barriers, and a host of other negative emotions, turning teachers away from engaging with assessment in meaningful ways that inform instruction and guide curricular decisions. In this chapter, we provide a path for educators to navigate their existing assessment landscape to make space for assessments that fill in the gaps about who their students are and what they know while still implementing required assessments. As Cardi B (2017) reminds us, we do not have to choose: we can do both.

In our work with teachers, we start by disrupting negative or limiting views of assessments by positioning assessment in the simplest terms: tools to get to know who students are, what students know and value, and data to inform instructional decisions. We recognize this isn't how assessment is typically approached in schools, but it's imperative that we *begin* here. We want educators to understand that assessments can provide valuable data about our students beyond a bubble sheet of answers, an oral reading score, or a proficiency rating. We teach educators to see assessment as useful and necessary for informing culturally responsive instructional decisions and as tools to gather information about students' identities, funds of knowledge, and lives. We model how teachers can be agentic in the area of assessment and make decisions about which assessments to use, what purpose the assessment will serve in guiding culturally responsive instructional decisions, and how to view assessment as *not one more thing*. So how do we define assessment and view assessment through a culturally responsive lens?

Drawing on Dewey's (2018) notion of inquiry, we view culturally responsive assessment as inquiry. Inquiry has long been a part of teaching and learning (Deboer, 2006; Hall, 2009; Harste, 2000; Lazonder & Harmsen, 2016) and utilized across disciplines as a model for curriculum (Harste & Vasquez, 2017; Spires et al., 2016) and to improve teacher practice (Hall, 2009; Han et al., 2017; Paseka et al., 2023). Inquiry requires learners to critically reflect and actively engage in learning. Using inquiry as a model for assessment positions teachers as active investigators who gather information about their students. This stance enables teachers to enact agency throughout the assessment process, affirm their students' identities and lived experiences by selecting the right tools, analyze data through an affirming lens, and utilize culturally affirming and responsive data to inform their literacy instructional decisions. Lazonder and Harmsen (2016) advocate for guidance when introducing inquiry and learning to use inquiry through simulation and practice. In the practical application section of this chapter, Anne presents ways to use guidance in inquiry so that educators can learn how to actively take up assessment as inquiry, be agentic in their assessment decisions, and overcome systemic barriers related to assessment.

Before we can teach teachers to implement assessment in this way, we must first guide them through the first component of our framework to evaluate their own beliefs about assessment and (re)evaluate the assessment systems already in place in their classrooms, schools, districts, states, and beyond. In other words, we begin this work by disrupting traditional conceptions of assessment and what (mis)conceptions educators may hold about their value and role in education.

Then we position teachers as the experts in learning about who students are, what they know, and what they need to continue learning, which is the second component in our framework. By advocating that teachers need to first learn about their students before they begin planning instruction for them (the third component of our framework), this ensures that educators are building on students' existing knowledge, experiences, and strengths in their curriculum. It also positions educators to see students through a culturally responsive lens, affirm their student identities and cultural knowledge, and guide all their decisions and interactions with their students through this lens.

Approaching assessment from this stance enables teachers to be agentic throughout the assessment process with the autonomy and authority to generate data to inform their literacy instructional decisions. For many of our practicing teachers, approaching assessment from an inquiry stance is liberating and sometimes unsettling. Knowing this, we are explicit and direct in how we model our thinking process through a culturally responsive lens so we can support them in making decisions about assessment in their own classrooms.

DISRUPTING SCENARIOS

In the opening scenario, Mr. Higgins uses literacy assessment to inform his reading instruction, but he is only gleaning surface information about his students' reading knowledge and interests. By using the required DIBELS and oral reading assessments, he is gaining valuable information about the discrete skills his students know, but not information he needs to plan literacy instruction that will engage and motivate his students. What is missing in his assessments are his students: who they are and what their lived experiences are. As Ladson-Billings has reminded us for nearly three decades, culturally responsive teachers "utilize students' culture as a vehicle for learning" (1995, p. 161). Mr. Higgins needs to make space to fill in the gaps so he can better support his students' literacy knowledge while still implementing the required current assessments. Although this may at first sound daunting and difficult, making this space, even a few minutes a day, can be invaluable to teachers committed to enacting more affirming and culturally responsive instruction and allows pathways to more effective learning.

By viewing assessment as inquiry, Mr. Higgins can fill in these gaps with assessments that gather the information he is lacking about his students' identities and literacy knowledge. He can start by generating questions about what knowledge he is missing and start to think about how he may gather the information through assessments that are easily available and quick to implement with very little materials. Since Mr. Higgins is already using assessments to collect information about literacy skills and oral reading, the gaps he needs to fill are about his students' identities and interests outside of school, their reading preferences, and how their families use literacy at home. These three topics of inquiry could translate into assessments he can implement in a matter of minutes and throughout the day and week.

First, to collect information about his students about their out of school interests, Mr. Higgins could build in an opening activity using journal prompts about the time they spend outside of the school day when his students first come into the classroom. They could orally share a few of these each day, he could read them as they are writing them, or he could collect them at the end of the week. This would provide both an opening literacy activity as well as assessment data about their interests and identities.

To gather information about his students' reading preferences, Mr. Higgins could ask his students questions about their reading preferences and interests as they transition from outside to inside each morning or inside to outside each afternoon. This could be a way for students to line up (e.g., "All students who enjoy poetry, please line up" or "All students who dislike nonfiction, please line up"). Mr. Higgins could add a reading conference to his already in place oral reading assessment. By asking students to share their understanding of the reading, he could gain insight into how they were comprehending the text. With a quick, "Tell me what you read" prompt, he would gain insight into their comprehension in an interactive way. If the student missed an important detail, Mr. Higgins could quickly respond by asking additional questions or asking the child to reread part of the text. Mr. Higgins could also start closely observing his students' literacy behaviors during their independent work time to see how they interact and act during these times. He could watch for genre choices, topic selections, stamina, and a host of other activities related to literacy engagement.

Finally, Mr. Higgins could ask students and their families about their literacy practices at home. This could be in the form of a survey or questionnaire, during informal interactions and scheduled conferences, or as an Open House or Curriculum Night activity. Some questions might include: "What kinds of materials do you read at home? What kinds of writing do you use at home?

Do you make a shopping list or a to-do list? Do people in your family tell stories or jokes? Do they sing or listen to music?" Students could also generate their own questions to ask family members about their literacy interests and preferences then interview their family members. Then they could compare or contrast their family members' responses to their own responses.

Mr. Higgins can use the information from each of these assessments to better inform the instructional materials he selects, the prompts he uses in instruction, and in the pedagogical choices he makes in his literacy instructional decisions. He can also use this information to interrupt and correct any misconceptions or stereotypes he may have about his students' literacy knowledge and/or how their families use literacy in their daily lives.

PRACTICAL APPLICATION

The following examples are from Anne who taught K–12 teachers enrolled in a two-course sequence about literacy assessment and a practicum course as part of a literacy education graduate program. Although these courses were designed for practicing teachers, I (Anne) provide examples of how similar activities could work with preservice teachers. These activities were taught in the sequence presented, which operationalized each of the five components of our framework. In both courses, I guided teachers to engage in an inquiry-based approach to learn about literacy assessment as inquiry. I used prompts, guiding questions, and scaffolding through simulation in the first course and in the second course teachers engaged in independent practice with planned check-ins with me and their colleagues.

The first part of the sequence was designed to guide teachers through disrupting pre-existing conceptions of assessment, including their own biases, and examining the current formative assessments in place in their educational context. Next, the exploration was followed by generating questions about student knowledge that could be answered by modifying existing assessments or including assessments not currently used. Then teachers engaged in an in-depth and self-directed study of alternative assessments that could fill these gaps or replace existing assessments to learn more about their students' identities, lived experiences, and their literacy knowledge. This process spanned over several weeks and culminated with an assessment plan based on their students and specific to their educational context. The goal was for educators to take an agentic approach to reimagine assessment through a culturally responsive lens in their teaching contexts.

The next part of the sequence was to implement their assessment plan, analyze the data using a culturally responsive lens, plan instruction based on the data analysis, and then implement culturally responsive literacy instruction using a case study approach. The goal of this activity was to take action and initiate change. The final part of this sequence included an action plan for sustaining the revised assessment plan within their educational context and reflecting on these changes within the community of learners in the course. Throughout the two courses, teachers worked with each other to collaborate, give and receive feedback, and reflect about each step of the multi-step process.

PART ONE OF THE SEQUENCE

The first part of the sequence was designed for educators to investigate the current assessment process, including tools and practices already in place in their educational context, disrupt the current plan, and propose a new assessment plan that was more inclusive and affirming for their students. Since this was a graduate course, many of the students were already in classrooms, homeschool teachers, or working with students in their community. For the educators not in classrooms or working within the community, their task was to investigate the assessments in place in a local school by interviewing a classroom teacher. If they did not have access to a classroom teacher, I put them in touch with a teacher in the area. The final two options could be used with preservice teachers not in classrooms. I provided them four prompts to organize the information they collected:

1. Current literacy assessments used
2. Brief description of each assessment
3. Purpose(s) of each assessment
4. Brief description of how data is currently used from each assessment

Based on the gathered information, I asked educators to reflect on the effectiveness of the assessment plan. I asked them to consider effectiveness in terms of providing useful, timely data and of providing data to plan culturally responsive and affirming literacy instruction. Oftentimes, teachers would report that they did not have access to the data in a timely manner, the data was too general (results of proficiency), only showed deficits, and/or the data was not useful in planning culturally responsive literacy instruction due to many unknowns about their students' ways of knowing, identities, and lived experiences. For educators not in their own classroom, I asked them to interview the classroom teacher using the above prompts. Educators were also prompted to become critical consumers of the assessments by considering the following questions about assessments using Muhammad (2023) as a guide:

- Who benefits from these assessments most?

- What is the historical data around these assessments (i.e., Who is doing well on them? Who isn't? Why?)
- Why do students of color historically score lower on these assessments?
- How are these assessments contributing to gaps in opportunity and equity?

After this discussion, I asked teachers to reflect on the gaps in the knowledge they have about their students. I also asked them about the types of information they would like to know about their students as well as how they could obtain the information through alternative formative assessments. When I introduce this concept, teachers often respond in fear that I am asking them to do more by adding to their already too cramped time with their students. I assure them that this is not the goal; the goal is to identify gaps in our knowledge about the students we teach. I remind teachers that if we are more knowledgeable about our students, we can be more effective teachers and have a greater impact on their learning. Then I introduce the assessment as inquiry cycle as a tool for generating questions, selecting tools to

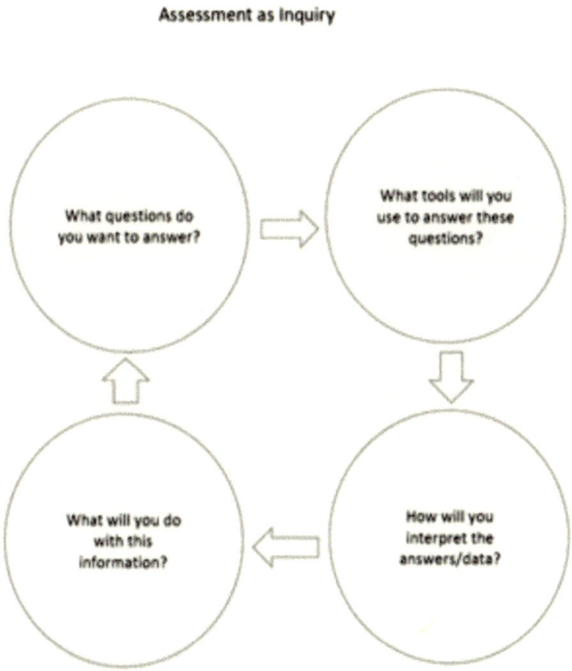

Assessment as Inquiry

```
What questions do    →    What tools will you
you want to answer?       use to answer these
                          questions?
        ↑                          ↓
What will you do     ←    How will you
with this                 interpret the
information?              answers/data?
```

Figure 3.1 Assessment as Inquiry Cycle
Anne Ticknor

find answers (or partial answers), analyzing the data, then planning next steps (figure 3.1).

Using this cycle as a model, I guide educators through a multi-week simulation of analyzing their current assessment plan to develop a more culturally affirming literacy assessment plan for their educational context. We start by collectively and individually reflecting on the gaps in their current assessment plans and start generating what data is missing about who their students are and what their students know about literacy. I ask educators, "What else would you need to know about your students to be more culturally responsive in your literacy instruction? What data would you need to affirm your students' identities and lived experiences in your instruction? Where are the gaps in your knowledge about your students' literacy strengths?"

Then I introduce a collection of readings about literacy assessment as a way to center equity in literacy curriculum and instruction (textbox 3.1). Educators reflect on these readings using the following guidance: "When you are reading, take note of items that are new to you and ideas that you were already familiar with as well as concepts that seem in contradiction to practices in your local context." The goal is for them to identify places in their current assessment plan where gaps could be filled by generating new questions.

While educators were reading this collection, we began brainstorming questions about what literacy knowledge students bring to us, and how they

---

TEXTBOX 3.1 COLLECTION OF READINGS

- First read *"I am Here for the Hard Re-set: Post Pandemic Pedagogy to Preserve Our Culture"* (https://drive.google.com/file/d/1Sw0khRPKRWythjAktA2YdGCojiSG8X65/view) by Dr. Gloria Ladson-Billings. In this article, Ladson-Billings describes the importance of culturally relevant pedagogy in an era of pandemic teaching. Ladson-Billings calls for a "hard re-set" in schools and focuses on several areas for re-setting including assessment. Start with this article.
- Read "The Critical Story of the 'Science of Reading' and Why Its Narrow Plotline Is Putting Our Children and Schools at Risk" (https://ncte.org/blog/2020/10/critical-story-science-reading-narrow-plotline-putting-children-schools-risk/) by Dr. Dorothy C. Suskind about the narrowing of what counts as reading.
- Read *"The Culturally Responsive Teacher"* (https://pdo.ascd.org/lmscourses/PD13OC002/media/Module6_Culturally

ResponsiveTeacher.pdf) by Dr. Ana María Villegas and Dr. Tamara Lucas about being culturally responsive teachers.
- Read *"Cultural Responsiveness and Engagement in Classrooms"* (https://assets.savvas.com/asset_mgr/current/202047/Ernest_Morrell_Whitepaper.pdf) by Dr. Ernest Morrell about the importance of cultural responsiveness and engagement in classrooms.
- Read *"Expecting Too Much—and Too Little?—of Literacy Teachers"* (https://writenow.nwp.org/toomuchtoolittle-b9372407053f) by Shawna Coppola about expecting too much—and too little—of literacy teachers.
- Read "Assessment as an Act of Love" (https://www.ascd.org/el/articles/assessment-as-an-act-of-love) by Christina Torres.

know it. I guide educators to consider literacy in holistic ways that include but also go beyond decoding and encoding printed text and encourage them to consider other ways of making meaning and communicating with others. To prompt their reflection, I ask educators, "What do your students know about the world and how do they communicate it with others? What do you want to know about how they have learned literacy up to this point so that you can build on their knowledge and help them grow in their knowledge? What about their identities would be helpful to know so that you can support their literacy growth? And, what about their lived experiences would help you make more culturally responsive and affirming instructional decisions?"

After educators generate their own individual list of questions, we begin an exploration of common literacy assessment tools and resources, which would support the second question in the assessment as inquiry cycle model: "What tools will you use to answer your questions?" I collected resources so that we have a common language about literacy assessments that might help them answer their questions with resources including readings, examples, and demonstrations for kidwatching (Souto-Manning et al., 2010), reading and writing interviews (Goodman et al., 2005), reading conferences (Krulder, 2018), Running Records (Barone et al., 2020), qualitative spelling inventories (Bear et al., 2020), and phonological awareness (Yopp & Yopp, 2009). The collection includes formative assessment tools that can be used across multiple grade levels and contexts and use very few materials. The collected assessments can be adapted to suit the educational context or need and can be implemented within a matter of minutes. In other words, the collection is meant to be easily accessible, and teachers have agency in their use to select based on the questions they generated.

After self-directed exploration of the resources educators are encouraged to select two or three of these assessments for their new assessment plan based on the questions they are seeking to answer. Although some of the assessments are familiar, others are not. Once I knew which assessments needed more practice or information, I included additional resources and individual meetings with educators for additional support in understanding and using the tool so educators could make well-informed decisions when considering which tools would best answer their questions. Our framework encourages social action in community with others, so I built that into the process by encouraging like or similar grade or content teachers to work together to finetune their assessment selections and questions.

As a group and individually, we also discussed practical considerations of adding or revising a current assessment plan. Teachers may be concerned that these would be additional items to add into their already too full daily to-do list. We discussed how these assessments would *not be one more thing*, they would be part of daily interactions and practices to learn more about their students. I reminded them that several of the assessments (interviews and conferences) could be worked into the daily activities already in place in their educational practice. For example, we discussed how elementary educators could interview their students while standing in line waiting for the lunchroom to open, or when meeting students after recess or another class. Secondary teachers could talk with their students informally about their reading or writing interests when checking in on their assignment progress or as class openers. We also discussed how if they already implemented journals or writing prompts, questions could be included about lived experiences or identities and writing samples could be analyzed using a spelling feature guide (Bear et al., 2020). The goal, I reminded them, was to add depth and breadth to the data they were already collecting about their students and not to add additional activities.

As we continued through the simulation of the cycle, we moved to the third question: "How will you interpret the answers/data?" I guided educators to view assessment data through a strengths-based and affirming lens and not through a deficit lens. This was a challenge for some of the practicing teachers since they were often coached to look at what students did not know and fill those gaps with instruction. I supported them to look at data in chunks and not as a whole. For example, educators may already implement a record of oral reading; however, they may have learned to see a word read incorrectly or correctly and not taught how to analyze how the miscue was made (e.g., read the word "home" as "house").

Since this is a simulation and they were in a community of learners, I encourage educators to slow down and not move to the instruction part too quickly. I guide them to challenge deficit thinking and disrupt their biases and assumptions about student literacy knowledge. To do this, I use Wager et al. (2019) to guide our practice by using their frames:

- Possible teacher assumptions
- Challenge these assumptions with realistic reasons
- Adopt a strengths-based lens

I also use examples from Wager et al.'s book to guide how to do this. Here is one example from their book about a student named Omar:

- Omar is not interested in learning. (Possible teacher assumptions.)
- Omar doesn't seem interested because he is tired. Perhaps he has responsibilities at home that keep him from getting enough sleep each night. (Challenge these assumptions with realistic reasons.)
- Omar is responsible and takes care of his younger siblings at home. (Adopt a strengths-based lens.)

I then use this model to share an example from one of my former fifth grade students, Harley, and how I had a brief conference with him to learn more about him. Harley was a very smart student who sometimes fell asleep in class and did not complete his homework. He always had the right answer in class discussions and he often shared his thinking as a model to his classmates. At first, I thought maybe he was not doing his homework because he did not want to complete it. Then I talked to Harley. Harley was one of five children at home, and he was the second youngest. He was responsible for getting his kindergarten-aged sister to and from school and helping her with her schoolwork after school. I also found out when talking with Harley that he and his older siblings were helping their father add on to their house in the evenings and weekends. He was learning skills in carpentry and construction while adding valuable space to their home. Finally, I found out my assumptions were wrong; Harley was interested in school and he did want to further his learning by completing his homework, however his evening and weekend responsibilities needed his attention. Once I learned all of this and what time the construction started after his dad returned home from work, I asked his parents if he and his younger sister could spend an extra forty-five minutes in my classroom to complete their homework and have an after-school snack. Since they walked home after school to their house a few blocks away, transportation was not an issue and their parents agreed. Had I not asked Harley about his lived experiences and his responsibilities outside of my classroom, I may have continued deficit-based assumptions, not seen his strengths and values, and enacted harm.

The final component of the assessment as inquiry cycle is for educators to consider what they will do with the new information the assessment results provided. We discussed the possibilities this would allow educators in their contexts and how the next steps usually included instruction and continuing the cycle by generating new questions. Once we were at this point of the course, I provided the following prompts for educators to develop a revised assessment plan:

- Name the current assessment to *revise* (delivery, format, etc.) or replace.
  - Name the new tool, if replacing.
- Brief rationale for the revision OR change (connect to your assessment resources).
- Answer *new* or *revised* questions with new or revised tool.
- Describe how data will be newly interpreted and used to better recognize students' strengths and build on their brilliance. This description should all be strength focused.
- Reflect on your assessment as inquiry cycle journey and name two or three ways that your perspective has changed about assessment.

Since this was a simulation, educators had the option to imagine a world where they could replace existing formative assessments that did not contribute meaningful data for making culturally responsive instructional decisions or did not add value in terms of timing and access to data. For many educators, this was not an option. Instead, they were able to use this opportunity to add an assessment that filled a gap in their knowledge about their students. For example, one educator revised their current practice to add a reading conference after conducting an oral reading assessment. Their reasoning was that this would offer valuable insight into the student's reading comprehension as well as the strategies they used to decode words in the reading. The reading conference would also add information about their reading preferences and identity as a reader. Another educator also revised a current practice of collecting a spelling sample by including a conference to ascertain students' metacognitive practices in spelling unknown or unfamiliar words. A third educator elected to incorporate prompts into their class opener about student interests outside of school to learn more about their students' lived experiences and identities. Several educators added kidwatching, or closely observing their student's literacy behaviors (Owocki & Goodman, 2002), into their daily routines so that they could intentionally observe how their students interacted with literacy in their classrooms. One educator shared that they were adding kidwatching because they had not been intentional in observing their students while independently reading or writing and this was an opportunity to do so. Each of these revisions were then put into practice in the practicum course as well as engaging in the remainder of our framework.

PART TWO OF THE SEQUENCE

In the second part of the two-course sequence, educators continued their assessment as inquiry cycle journey by moving from simulation to practice and implementing their assessment plan as a case study with one to three students in their teaching context. For educators who were not currently in an educational context, they either partnered with a classroom teacher or worked with students in their community to implement the case study. Had they been preservice teachers, they would have completed the case study in an assigned practicum classroom. The goal of the case study was to implement and complete the assessment as inquiry cycle, plan literacy instructional lessons, then reflect about the students' growth and their own growth.

Educators adapted their assessment plan from the first course to fit the time of the school year and then create a timeline for implementation of each part of the cycle. I lead this discussion by asking educators to consider their breaks, how much class time they could realistically devote to the tasks, and then guide them to refine their assessment plan to include two or three assessments that could seamlessly be added to their existing schedules.

In each step of the case study, educators included rationales for their decisions and reflected on their decisions based on the course readings and resources. They were guided to write from a strengths-based, affirming lens about each student, refrain from using deficit language, and build on what

---

TEXTBOX 3.2 CULTURALLY RESPONSIVE AND AFFIRMING DATA ANALYSIS PROMPTS

Use the following sets of questions to extend the data analysis with a specific lens for this course:

- First, consider these questions for each student using the data you collected:
  - What does this data tell me about my student's identities?
  - What does this data tell me about my student's cultural knowledge or funds of knowledge?
  - What does this data tell me about my student's literacy strengths?

- Then answer the next set of questions about each student:
  - What did you learn about their identities?
  - What did you learn about their cultural knowledge and/or funds of knowledge?
  - What did you learn about their literacy strengths? Consider as appropriate: reading (decoding and comprehension), writing (sentence structure, vocabulary use, grammar, spelling, conventions, ideas), speaking, listening, etc.
- Finally, **define instructional goals** for each student based on their assessment results using the final set of questions:
  - How are these goals inclusive of and build on their identities?
  - How are these goals inclusive of and build on their cultural knowledge and/or funds of knowledge?
  - How are these goals inclusive of and build on their literacy strengths?

Remember,
- Write using asset language (see Wager et al., 2019)
- Avoid using labels and deficit or coded language (see Ticknor et al., 2021)

they already knew about the student(s). For example, one educator described a student selected for the case study as engaged in class discussions, interested in asking questions, and enjoys math, and another educator described their student as a sports enthusiast who spends hours outside of school traveling with their sports team.

Since the first course simulated many of these tasks and pieces of the case study, my feedback often was in the form of guidance and encouragement to individuals with several planned check-in points during the case study. This was planned so that they could get and give feedback to their classmates, engage in discussions about what was working and what was challenging, revise their plans as needed, and build community with their colleagues. I structured these check-in points and created discussion prompts to encourage educators to build knowledge and confidence about the changes they were enacting in their educational contexts. I asked educators to collaborate on their thinking, support each other in making space for assessments that were more inclusive of their students' knowledge, and encourage each other to take risks that helped them learn more about themselves, their students, and being more culturally affirming and responsive educators.

When educators moved to the data analysis portion of the case study, I provided them with prompts to guide their analysis (textbox 3.2).

In the first course, we practiced analysis through simulation, and they worked in small groups. In this course, I wanted to provide them additional support as they analyzed data they had collected themselves from their students and considered how the results could be used to make literacy instructional goals and plans. I encouraged educators to use the language examples from Wager et al. (2019), our first book (Ticknor et al., 2021), and other examples from published works. I also offered sentence frames, such as "My student can . . . ," "My student knows . . . ," and "My student understands . . . ," so they had a concrete model for writing from a strengths-based stance.

Central to the analysis prompts was an emphasis on identity and ways of knowing through cultural knowledge and funds of knowledge. Moll et al. describes funds of knowledge as "historically accumulated and culturally developed bodies of knowledge and skills essential for household or individual functioning and well-being" and how members "use their funds of knowledge in dealing with changing, and often difficult, social and economic circumstances" (2006, p. 133). Centering these concepts as part of the data to be analyzed prepares educators to consider not only what a student knows about literacy but also how they know and use it, which can be helpful in planning more affirming and responsive literacy instruction that builds on students' strengths. The final step of the analysis was to write instructional goals based on the data results. To write the goals, teachers were to identify strengths from the assessments and to use accurate and affirming language to describe what the student knows. I prompted educators to consider, "What literacy knowledge did my student demonstrate? How can I build on this knowledge? How can I use their identities and cultural knowledge to build on their existing literacy knowledge?" I also provided guidance for educators to write these from a strength-based and affirming stance with sentence frames:

- Based on the (name the assessment) results . . . I learned that . . .
- The instructional goal will build on (name strength) by . . . and affirm the students' (identities, cultural knowledge, funds of knowledge) by . . .

Once instructional goals were established, educators created literacy lessons based on the goals using culturally affirming and responsive pedagogy and instructional materials. Since we expand on these components and offer extensive strategies in the previous chapters of this book and our previous book, which provides several examples, I only will provide the prompting questions I used to encourage educators to connect data to lesson planning and material selection here:

- What did you learn about your students' identities that can be affirmed in your instructional decisions?
- What did you learn about your students' interests and lived experiences that can inform your instructional materials choices?
- How can you build on your students' literacy knowledge with this method of instruction?
- How will the material selection motivate and interest this student?
- How are your decisions based on the data you collected?

An example of a rationale for instructional planning from one of the educators follows:

> In our Reading Conference, the student explained that he loves to read books about other cultures and religions that are different from his. He also loves mysteries. I kept that in mind when choosing the texts for him to read. The student also comes from a family that is very supportive of reading and he looks up to his sister because she is the type of reader he wants to be. Since he comes from a family that supports his interests and motivation with reading, I knew teaching him strategies to monitor his comprehension was the right way to go. The student is eager to learn ways to improve, which comes from the culture around reading that his family has set for him.

After each lesson, educators were prompted to reflect on what they learned about their students and about themselves, which are the first two components of our framework. I included the following questions as prompts: "What did you learn about your students' literacy strengths? How will you continue to build on these strengths? What did you learn about your students' identities and cultural knowledge? How will you continue to build on these strengths? What did you learn about yourself as a culturally responsive and affirming literacy educator? How will you continue to build on your learning?"

At each check-in point of the case study, educators are prompted to reflect on their own learning and growth as literacy educators. Their reflections were part of what they were to share with their classmates, and this provided a connection to build community and learn together. I wanted educators to learn from each other about what resonated for them, expanding their conceptions about assessment, and shaping their practices as teachers. I also wanted them to know they were in a community of co-conspirators who were allies in enacting change to reduce harm to students in a manner that was sustainable.

Throughout the two-course sequence, I also brought in several practicing teachers as virtual guest lecturers from several different states and grade levels, ranging from kindergarten to secondary settings. Each teacher shared the questions they investigate through assessment, the assessments they use and how they selected them, and the kinds of information they learn about their students' identities, interests, lived experiences, and cultural knowledge in their specific classroom contexts. Several of the guest lecturers shared sample assessments, talked through data analysis, provided real examples of how they fit in assessments into the existing assessment plans in their contexts, and how they use the assessment data in their instructional planning. Having the opportunity to talk with real teachers who are using assessments in this way provides additional insight and modeling of how this can be done in classroom settings. Evidence of the impact of these guest lecturers was also demonstrated in the rationales for the assessment plans in the first course and the case studies in the second course.

For some of the educators in the two-course sequence, they were in positions to impact change in the assessment plan for their schools. They served in instructional coach roles and had the ability to make changes to current practices. They had the ear of the administration, and they had the data to support why a change would benefit students at their school. Other educators in the courses were able to enact change in their grade levels or content teams by filling the gaps in their current assessment plans and adding assessments that provide additional information about their students. All educators in the course had access to new tools and resources so that they could navigate their current assessment plan and sustain change in their individual teaching contexts to better educate their students through affirming and culturally responsive practices.

CONCLUSION

In this chapter we offered educators ways to make space for culturally affirming and responsive assessment and to view assessment as inquiry. We want educators to feel supported in filling the gaps left by required literacy assessments that may not include learning about who students are and how they know about literacy. As evidenced in our framework, our goal is to center students' identities and their lived experiences in our classroom practices. This starts with teachers examining themselves and the systems they work in and ends with working to enact change within a community of co-conspirators. We hope that this chapter provides guidance for educators to make space to do this work in their literacy assessments. As we close this chapter, we want to offer readers a window into our intentional and deliberate thinking about assessment with a few more questions for reflection.

STOP AND REFLECT

- What does "assessment" mean to you?
- What are your experiences (as a student, as a teacher) with assessment?
- How can your view, or your experiences, about assessment be extended to include culturally affirming and responsive assessment practices?
- What are the current assessments in place in your educational context?
- What purpose does each assessment serve, and what data are you able to glean from it?
- What information about your students are you missing? Where are the gaps in your knowledge about your students?
- What questions could you answer if you made space for new literacy assessments?
- How will you make this space? What strategies could you try from these examples or what new strategies could work in your context?
- How will you use this new data in your instructional planning?
- How will you sustain making space for culturally affirming and responsive literacy assessments?
- Who will be your community of co-conspirators and provide support when enacting change?

Chapter 4

It's Not "One More Thing": It's the Only Thing

Somehow this book felt more difficult to write than the last one, which surprised the three of us. After all, we wrote the last book at the height of COVID-19 and during a time when our hearts were wrapped in pain, anger, and disappointment as we reeled in the aftermath of the murder of George Floyd. Yet this time, our challenges were different. We were different, with different roles and different responsibilities. We were continuing to learn and unlearn around ideas of racism, healing, and justice in our practices. This time we were reflecting on harm in our education systems, our role in education systems, and the constant flow of oppressive laws and policies that flooded our inboxes and newsfeeds. While at the same time, we were (and still are) carrying the pain, anger, and disappointment that we faced in the chaos of 2020. The writing process was heavy and easy to avoid.

Through the struggle, we decided to embrace our challenges, our world, our systems, and continue to consider how we could push back against the constant flow of oppression and injustice in education. We were determined to continue to find and share ways that validate and center children. Children are the very reason we engage in this work. Affirming their identities, funds of knowledge, and brilliance in the face of systems that try to silence and erase them is central to our work and we recognize it is our responsibility to push through and push back in order to ensure their best interests are centered in and outside of classrooms. As Muhammad reminds us, "If we are not centering children's humanity through love, there is no strategy, no professional book or instructional method in the world that can prepare the teacher to elevate the child" (2023, p. 15). Each chapter in this book centers children, their identities, their experiences, their brilliance. Each chapter in this book encourages educators to examine what and how they teach in order to center the lives and experiences of children. We agree, there is no strategy, book, or method that can prepare a teacher to engage in this work if they are unable to center the humanity of children and embrace the mindset of equity and justice in our educational systems. Regardless of our challenges and changes, this stance has remained the same.

A lot of things have changed since our last book. On the brink of tenure, Mikkaka found herself questioning her path. Like many people, she'd done a lot of reflecting and growing during the pandemic, and her priorities had shifted. So, she left academia behind and found more peace (and more money) in the nonprofit world. She took her own advice and created space for rest, creativity, and rejuvenation, so that she could keep doing good work without burning out. She's found herself living a much more balanced life, one that prioritizes her own wellness.

Still, she has a teacher's heart and the ancestors' whispers in her ears, reminding her that she must leave this world better than she found it. And so she continues advocating for equity in education through a variety of work projects, such as leading equity reviews, facilitating educator learning communities, and writing a monthly equity-focused literacy blog. She's also still working with teachers, as a part-time instructor.

Meanwhile, Anne also found herself thinking about needing a pivot in her professional life. During the pandemic, she became increasingly involved in the university's faculty senate and decided to run for chair of the faculty. She was elected and then re-elected for a second term. Although she enjoys much of this new role, it is temporary and requires a break from several of her usual faculty responsibilities, including teaching and scholarship. The time she once had with university students has now been replaced with time spent with faculty and administrators. The time she spent giving presentations and writing about culturally responsive literacy instruction is now spent on presentations about shared governance, university policies, and providing remarks across the university and state. Anne's new job means quicker access to state and university policies, laws impacting higher education, and the ability to be involved in these conversations around them.

Even though this has been a shift in responsibilities, Anne has stayed committed to culturally affirming and responsive instruction by carving out space to mentor students, write this book, run a long delayed educational program affirming Indigenous voices in American history, and keep up with research projects related to equity and inclusion. Anne has learned to be more deliberate in making time in her schedule to enable these activities to occur. Although each of these activities may not be centered on literacy instruction, the focus remains on affirming the identities and lived experiences of the communities she is working within.

Christy has taken on leadership roles within her department, and she continues to consider how she can support students and their educational experiences. While she conducts research on the experiences of students of color in educational spaces, she recognizes that action must be a part of this process as well. Her research led her to create an affinity group for students of color. This is a space for students to celebrate their shared identities, interests, and experiences. This is also a place of peace, love, liberation, affirmation, and support. In this space students' identities are validated, their experiences are shared, and they have a safe space to show up as their authentic selves.

Christy has mentored preservice teachers in honors programs as they create resources for educators to find and utilize diverse books in their classrooms. Realizing that finding financial support for diverse books and effective professional development can be a barrier, Christy also works in spaces with school and district leaders, providing professional development on how to support teachers in creating inclusive, antiracist curriculum. She has also written grants to add diverse books in K–8 classrooms. With each of these actions, we believe we are moving closer to our goals of change, learning with and from K–12 educators, students, and leaders. We do not sit in the tower or behind our desks, naive to the realities of what is happening in classrooms. We are actively working with classroom teachers, school leaders, and policy advocates to ensure we are aware of the challenges facing K–12 education and we are poised to act as needed (figure 4.1).

Although we have all shifted in our roles and responsibilities, we have not changed our commitment to equity in education. We each enact our

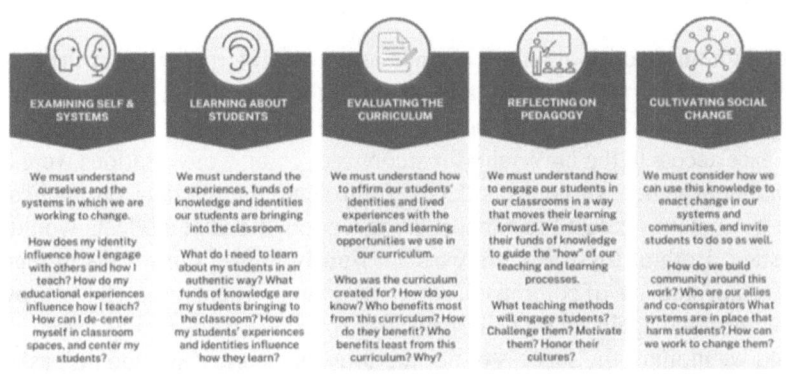

Figure 4.1 Culturally affirming and responsive framework for transformative instruction: It's not one more thing.
Mikkaka Overstreet

framework in the educational spaces we are part of with the ultimate goal of transforming education because it is the lens that our interactions pass.

We have found that we need to be more intentional to be in the same physical space now that our daily work lives have altered; however, we know that we will always share a drive to save education, in whatever small ways we can. That's why, when Christy texted us that she needed to talk, we were all on a virtual call within the hour.

Christy wanted to process the ruling from SCOTUS about the Fair Admissions Act (*Students for Fair Admissions, Inc. v. President and Fellows of Harvard College*, 2023). Soon after the decision was made, our state university system issued guidance (Division of Legal Affairs, 2023). Included on the fifth page of the guidance is,

> CONSIDER THE DECISION'S EFFECT ON OTHER PRACTICES. It is likely that Students for Fair Admissions' holding and rationale will be extended to other instances where university actors use race in allocating university resources. Because the rationale of the decision could affect the award of scholarships and financial aid, campuses should begin to evaluate and assess any scholarship or aid programs that consider race in the award of the benefit, and the extent to which campus officials play a role in the award decision. Institutions should broadly consider how various University-sponsored programs are constituted and organized. Programs that offer opportunities for students based on race to the exclusion of others, who are not of the same race, may also be implicated by the Court's ruling. So, too, campuses should start evaluating whether they believe certain scholarships, aid, and campus programs are still permissible.

Although many critiqued the guidance as an overinterpretation of the ruling (Killian, 2023), our university and others in the state began quickly revising programs, scholarships, and a host of other initiatives designed to support and increase access to the university for students of color. Conversations were had debating whether we could collect certain demographic data on applicants and how groups created to support diverse populations of students would be affected. Both of these matters would seriously impact our efforts to recruit and retain students of color in education programs, where research has proved time and time again, there is a great need for a diverse teaching force. How could we monitor the success of our recruitment efforts if we couldn't ask for racial/ethnic identity? How could we improve retention if we couldn't create and name spaces and support systems specifically for marginalized students?

Adherence to this decision and guidance feels like a massive step back for higher education institutions and the students we seek to serve. Already, people are removing the carefully crafted antiracism statements that were so popular in 2020 from their university's web pages. Universities across the country are removing DEI content, courses, and entire programs based on recent state laws. K–12 schools are also feeling pressure to scrub away efforts to make education more accessible and inclusive of their students and teachers. In the state in which we live, the governor has declared a State of Emergency for Public Education (North Carolina Governor's Office, 2023) and called for legislators to reconsider legislation that would severely impact the public education system and harm those it serves. Across the nation it feels like we are quickly losing so much of the slow progress we've made toward ensuring the educational system is safer, less harmful, and more inclusive for people from marginalized communities.

However, we cannot help but to wonder if it was really progress or performative discourse. The anger and uprisings after the murder of George Floyd made us believe this was a time of change, a time of reckoning, where the nation realized we should be teaching through an antiracist lens, we should be making visible the inequities in our educational systems, and we should be discussing the ways in which we had harmfully failed our students and in essence our society by not doing these things. We saw antiracist educators, researchers, and authors being discussed or giving interviews on every major television network. We were fired up and ready to work toward freedom, liberation, and antiracist teaching. We were ready to work to mend the harm and inequity with support from schools, districts, and corporations, until . . . until it became "too much," until people were tired of talking about it and tired of hearing about it and now, with new policies and laws, we are back to the harm, back to the inequitable policies dressed up as "fairness."

Fairness. Harm. Inequity. Access. These are words we used that day when Christy called and needed to process the implications of this law. The "Fair Admissions" Act is not fair if it doesn't take into account the disproportionate ways in which our K–12 education system is designed to foster a framework of the "haves and have nots." There are clear inequities in resources, teacher quality, and educational opportunities depending on your zip code. There are clear inequities in who can afford SAT tutoring, resources, and additional programs to prepare students for college entrance exams, interviews, essay writing, etc. All students do not have access to the resources they need. Knowing this, we know the "Fairness Act" is not fair. So why don't we start there instead of engaging in the harm of erasing race? Why don't we address the harm these inequities cause as students work toward applying for college (if they so choose)?

Why don't we fix these harmful policies and ensure all students have exactly what they need? Is it easier to pretend race does not exist in this process? Is it easier to erase students of color and their experiences? Is it easier to pretend that the "Fairness Act" is fair? No. No, it is not. We will not be fooled by performative discourse and laws and policies that are written to erase the beauty and brilliance of students in the name of fairness. We will not pretend that this is not an attack on recruitment efforts as we try to create diverse teacher pipelines, healing the harm that *Brown v. Board of Education* caused decades ago. But what we will do is act. We will create curriculum that works to amplify the voices and experiences of historically marginalized people, people who have been silenced because of their race, gender, sexual orientation, religion, or socioeconomic status. We will support educators as they work to repair the harm that decades of educational laws and policies have caused and continue to cause. We will work to show every student that they are valued, affirmed, loved, and supported. We will work to disrupt the systems that are in place that do not provide equitable access to all students. We will work to diversify the teacher workforce.

We are tired of talking about it. It's time to be about it. That's why our books focus on action. That's why we provide practical examples and approaches to the work. That's why we spent time writing another book while the world burned, our lives seemed way too busy to include writing together, and it felt like "one more thing"—even to us. Doing what's best for children, and thereby the future, in the face of overwhelming odds isn't one more thing. It's the only thing.

The current state of education in this country is not sustainable. No amount of laws, bans, mandates, and cookie-cutter required trainings are going to fix it. We have to recognize the structural barriers that prevent inclusive learning opportunities, like one-size-fits-all scripted curriculum. We have to push against these barriers and present and advocate for equitable approaches to teaching and learning, like culturally responsive instruction. In addition, we have to hold each other accountable in this process. We recognize we are all learning. None of us are without fault, but we hold each other accountable in this space of learning. We must ask each other questions, like the ones we pose in our "stop and reflect" sections of this book. "How does your current curriculum consider student identity, community, and experiences? What are the multiple opportunities you give students to showcase their knowledge on assignments and assessments?" We ask ourselves and each other these questions. We share ideas and thoughts for lesson and course revisions. We share new readings that influence our thinking and we consider ourselves as lifelong learners. This collaborative journey is one of learning and growth. It is a journey of learning how to best support and center our students. Muhammad reminds us that "the purpose of education is not to bolster our egos, but to ensure that students feel self-empowered, self-reliant, self-determined, and self-liberated" (2023, p. 25). If we truly believe this, we must enact this. We must ask ourselves how do we ensure that students feel self-empowered? Self-reliant? Self-determined? Self-liberated? If we do not have answers to these questions, we must transform our curriculum to address them. Education is power, it is determination, it is freedom. Our classrooms and instruction should reflect this. Our students deserve this. And so do our teachers, our communities, and our futures. If you are committed to ensuring the success of your students, your communities, and yourself and your colleagues as educators, join us on this journey to be about it. Approaching teaching through a culturally affirming and responsive lens isn't one more thing. It's the only thing.

References

Acevedo, E. (2020). *Clap when you land*. Harperteen.

African American art: Harlem renaissance, civil rights era, and beyond. (2012). Smithsonian American Art Museum. https://americanart.si.edu/exhibitions/african-american-2012

Ahmed, S. (2018). *Being the change: Lessons and strategies to teach social comprehension*. Heinemann.

A new African American identity: The Harlem renaissance. (2018). National Museum of African American History and Culture. https://nmaahc.si.edu/explore/stories/new-african-american-identity-harlem-renaissance

Archibald, S., Coggshall, J. G., Croft, A., & Goe, L. (2011). *High-quality professional development for all teachers: Effectively allocating resources*. National Comprehensive Center for Teacher Quality.

Barone, J., Khairallah, P., & Gabriel, R. (2020). Running records revisited: A tool for efficiency and focus. *The Reading Teacher, 73*(4), 525–30.

Bear, D., Invernizzi, M., Templeton, S. & Johnston, F. (2020). *Words their way: Word study for phonics, vocabulary, and spelling instruction* (6th ed.). Pearson.

Bishop, R. S. (1990). Mirrors, windows, and sliding glass doors. *Perspectives: Choosing and Using Books for the Classroom, 6*(3), ix–xi.

Cardi, B. (2017). Bodak yellow [Song]. On *Invasion of privacy* [Album]. Atlantic Records.

Case, A. (2015). Beyond the language barrier: Opening spaces for ELL/Non-ELL interaction. *Research in the Teaching of English, 49*(4), 361–82.

Coppola, S. (2019). *Expecting too much—and too little?—of literacy teachers*. NWP Write Now. https://writenow.nwp.org/toomuchtoolittle-b9372407053f

Darling-Hammond, L., Wei, R. C., Andree, A., Richardson, N., & Orphanos, S. (2009). *Professional learning in the learning profession*. National Staff Development Council.

Deboer, G. E. (2006). Historical perspectives on inquiry teaching in schools. In L. B. Flick & N. G. Lederman (Eds.), *Scientific inquiry and nature of science: Implications for teaching, learning, and teacher education* (pp. 17–35). Springer. https://george-deboer.org/wp-content/uploads/2020/10/Historical-Perspectives-on-Inquiry-Teaching-in-Schools.pdf

Desimone, L. M., Porter, A. C., Garet, M. S., Yoon, K. S., & Birman, B. F. (2002). Effects of professional development on teachers' instruction: Results from a three-year longitudinal study. *Educational Evaluation and Policy Analysis, 24*(2), 81–112.

Dewey, J. (2018). *Logic-The theory of inquiry*. Read Books.

Division of Legal Affairs (2023, August). *Directives regarding implementation of Student for Fair Admissions decision*. The University of North Carolina System. https://www.northcarolina.edu/wp-content/uploads/reports-and-documents/legal/unc-system-office-directives-regarding-implementation-of-students-for-fair-admissions-decision.pdf

Ebarvia, T. (2023). *Get free: Antibias literacy instruction for stronger readers, writers, and thinkers*. Corwin.

Finn, P. (2009). *Literacy with an attitude: Educating working class children in their own self-interest*. State University of New York Press.

Fitzgerald, E. (1956). Manhattan [Song]. On *Essential Ella* [Album]. Verve.

Fitzgerald, E. (1957). Drop Me off in Harlem [Song]. On *Ella Fitzgerald sings the Duke Ellington song book* [Album]. Verve.

Freire, P. (2000). *Pedagogy of the oppressed* (30th anniversary ed.). Continuum.

Friedman, J., & Tager, J. (2021). *Educational gag orders: Legislative restrictions on the freedom to read, learn, and teach*. Pen America. https://pen.org/report/educational-gag-orders/

Gay, G. (2010). *Culturally responsive teaching: Theory, research and practice* (2nd ed.). Teachers College Press.

Gay, G. (2013). Teaching to and through cultural diversity. *Curriculum Inquiry, 43*(1), 48–70.

Gay, G. (2018). *Culturally responsive teaching: Theory, research and practice* (3rd ed.). Teachers College Press.

Goodman, Y., Watson, D., & Burke, C. (2005). *Reading Miscue Inventory: From Evaluation to Instruction*, RC Owen, New York.

Good Morning America. (2023, January 21). *Ron DeSantis bans new AP African American studies class*. ABC News. https://abcnews.go.com/GMA/News/video/ron-desantis-bans-new-ap-african-american-studies-96580374

Guskey, T. (1997). Research needs to link professional development and student learning. *Journal of Staff Development, 18*, 36–41.

Guskey, T. (2002). Professional development and teacher change. *Teachers and Teaching: Theory and Practice, 8*(3), 381–91.

Hall, E. (2009). Engaging in and engaging with research: Teacher inquiry and development. *Teachers and Teaching: Theory and Practice, 15*(6), 669–81. https://www.doi.org/10.1080/13540600903356985

Han, S., Blank, J., & Berson, I. R. (2017). To transform or to reproduce: Critical examination of teacher inquiry within early childhood teacher preparation. *Journal of Early Childhood Teacher Education, 38*(4), 308–25.

Harriet Tubman Memorial stands as a symbol of fortitude and freedom in Harlem. (2014). Arts Observer. http://www.artsobserver.com/2012/02/19/harriet-tubman-memorial-stands-as-a-symbol-of-fortitude-and-freedom-in-harlem/

Harste, J. C. (2000). Six points of departure. In *Beyond reading and writing: Inquiry, curriculum, and multiple ways of knowing* (pp. 1–16). National Council of Teachers of English.

Harste, J. C., & Vasquez, V. M. (2017). What do we mean by literacy now?: Critical curricular implications. In *Global conversations in literacy research* (pp. 14–28). Routledge. http://jeromeharste.com/wp-content/uploads/2012/12/whatLnow.pdf

Hermann-Wilmarth, J. M. & Ryan, C. L. (2014). Doing What You Can: Considering Ways to Address LGBT Topics in Language Arts Curricula. Language Arts 92(6), 436–43.

Hermann-Wilmarth, J. M. (2020). Identity deficits: Reading, learning, and teaching trans and racial identities in an upper elementary classroom. In C. Mayo, & M. V. Blackburn (Eds.), *Queer, trans, and intersectional theory in educational practice: Student, teacher, and community experiences* (pp. 64–76). Routledge.

Hermann-Wilmarth, J., & Ryan, C. L. (2023). Queer Mothering in Academia as Pandemic Preparation: A Dialogue between QueerMotherScholarFriends. In Guyotte K. W., Shelton S. A., Melchior S., Coogler C. H. (Eds.), *Fabulating futures with academic mothers: Provocations for higher education* (pp. 141–55). Brill.

History of Times Square. (2017). Times Square NYC. https://www.timessquarenyc.org/history-of-times-square

Hughes, L. (n.d.). *Harlem by Langston Hughes*. Poetry Foundation. https://www.poetryfoundation.org/poems/46548/harlem

Hughes, L. (n.d.). *The negro speaks of rivers*. Poets.org. https://poets.org/poem/negro-speaks-rivers

Killian, J. (2023, August 23) *UNC System issues new directives after U.S. Supreme Court ruling on race in admissions*. NC Newsline. https://ncnewsline.com/2023/08/23/unc-system-issues-new-directives-after-u-s-supreme-court-ruling-on-race-in-admissions/

Krulder, J. (2018). *The unexpected power of reading conferences*. Edutopia. https://www.edutopia.org/article/unexpected-power-reading-conferences

Ladson-Billings, G. (1992). Reading between the lines and beyond the pages: A culturally relevant approach to literacy teaching. *Theory into Practice, 31*(4), 312–20.

Ladson-Billings, G. (1995). But that's just good teaching! The case for culturally relevant pedagogy. *Theory into Practice, 34*(3), 159–65.

Ladson-Billings, G. (2000). Fighting for our lives: Preparing teachers to teach African American students. *Journal of Teacher Education, 51*(3), 206–14.

Ladson-Billings, G. (2021). I'm here for the hard re-set: Post pandemic pedagogy to preserve our culture. *Equity & Excellence in Education, 54*(1), 68–78.

Lazarus, E. (n.d.). *The New Colossus by Emma Lazarus*. Poetry Foundation. https://www.poetryfoundation.org/poems/46550/the-new-colossus

Lazonder, A. W., & Harmsen, R. (2016). Meta-Analysis of inquiry-based learning: Effects of guidance. *Review of Educational Research, 86*(3), 681–718. https://doi.org/10.3102/0034654315627366

Lee, J. (2022, May 18). *Confronting the invisibility of anti-Asian racism*. Brookings. https://www.brookings.edu/articles/confronting-the-invisibility-of-anti-asian-racism/

Love, B. L. (2019). *We want to do more than survive: Abolitionist teaching and the pursuit of educational freedom*. Beacon Press.

Love, B. (2023). *Punished for dreaming: How school reform harms black children and how we heal*. St. Martin's Press.

Martinez-Neal, J. (2018). *Alma and how she got her name*. Candlewick Press.

McManis, C. W., & Sorell T. (2019). *Indian no more*. Tu Books.

Moll, L., Amanti, C., Neff, D., & Gonzalez, N. (2006). Funds of knowledge for teaching: Using a qualitative approach to connect homes and classrooms. In *Funds of knowledge* (pp. 71–87). Routledge.

Morrell, E. (2020). *Cultural responsiveness and engagement in classrooms*. Savvas Learning Company.

Morrissey, M. S. (2000). *Professional learning communities: An ongoing exploration*. Southwest Educational Development Laboratory.

Muhammad, G. (2020). *Cultivating genius: An equity framework for culturally and historically responsive literacy*. Scholastic.

Muhammad, G. (2023). *Unearthing joy: A guide to culturally and historically responsive teaching and learning*. Scholastic.

Muñiz, J. (2019). *Culturally responsive teaching: A 50-state survey of teaching standards*. New America.

National Governors Association Center for Best Practices, & Council of Chief State School Officers. (2010). *Common Core State Standards for English language arts & literacy in history/social studies, science, and technical subjects*.

North Carolina Governor's Office (2023). *A statement of emergency for public education*. State of North Carolina. https://governor.nc.gov/public-education-crisis

Novak, A. (2018). *Best practices in professional learning and teacher preparation in gifted education: Methods and strategies for gifted professional development* (Vol. 1). Sourcebooks.

Overstreet, M. (2017). Culture at the core: Moving from professional development to professional learning. *Journal of Ethnographic and Qualitative Research, 11*(3), 199–214.

Owocki, G., & Goodman, Y. (2002). *Kidwatching: Documenting children's literacy development*. Heinemann.

Paris, D., & Alim, H. S. (Eds.). (2017). *Culturally sustaining pedagogies: Teaching and learning for justice in a changing world*. Teachers College Press.

Paseka, A., Hinzke, J-H., & Boldt, V-P. (2023). Learning through perplexities in inquiry-based learning settings in teacher education. *Teachers and Teaching*. https://doi.org/10.1080/13540602.2023.2266379

Pendharkar, E. (2022, September 30). As book bans escalate, here's what you need to know. *Education Week*. https://www.edweek.org/teaching-learning/as-book-bans-escalate-heres-what-you-need-to-know/2022/09

Quintero, I. (2019). *My papi has a motorcycle*. Scholastic.

Ryan, C. L. & Hermann-Wilmarth, J. M. (2018). Reading the rainbow: LGBTQ inclusive literacy instruction in the elementary classroom.

Sealey-Ruiz, Y. (2022). An archaeology of self for our times: Another talk to teachers. *English Journal, 111*(5), 21–26.

Smagorinsky, P. (2018). Literacy in teacher education: "It's the context, stupid." *Journal of Literacy Research, 50*(3), 281–303.

Soto, G. (1995). *Oranges/Ode to family photographs*. Rubicon Books.

Souto-Manning, M., Mills, H., & O'Keefe, T. (2010). Teacher as Researcher: Collaborative Inquiry: From Kidwatching to Responsive Teaching. *Childhood Education, 86*(3), 169–71.

Spires, H. A., Kerkhoff, S. N., & Graham, A. C. (2016). Disciplinary literacy and inquiry: Teaching for deeper content learning. *Journal of Adolescent & Adult Literacy, 60*(2), 151–61.

Students for Fair Admissions, Inc. v. President and Fellows of Harvard College. 600 U.S. 20–1199 & 21–707 (2023). https://www.supremecourt.gov/opinions/22pdf/20-1199_hgdj.pdf

Suskind, D. (2020, October 24). *The critical story of the "science of reading" and why its narrow plotline is putting our children and schools at risk.* NCTE Blog. https://ncte.org/blog/2020/10/critical-story-science-reading-narrow-plotline-putting-children-schools-risk/

Swift, T. (2014). Welcome to New York [Song]. On *1989* [Album]. Big Machine.

Ticknor, A. S., Howard, C. M., & Overstreet, M. H. (2021). *It's not "one more thing": Culturally responsive and affirming strategies in K–12 literacy classrooms.* Rowman & Littlefield.

Torres, C. (2019, February 1). Assessment as an act of love. *ASCD* (61), 2. https://www.ascd.org/el/articles/assessment-as-an-act-of-love

U.S. Department of Education. (2018). *Civil rights data collection (CRDC) for the 2017–18 school year.* https://www2.ed.gov/about/offices/list/ocr/docs/crdc-2017-18.html

Vescio, V., Ross, D., & Adams, A. (2008). A review of research on the impact of professional learning communities on teaching practice and student learning. *Teaching and Teacher Education, 24*(1), 80–91.

Villegas, A. M., & Lucas, T. (2007). The culturally responsive teacher. *Educational Leadership, 64*(6), 28.

Wager, A. C., Clarke, L. W., & Enriquez, G. (2019). *The reading turn-around with emergent bilinguals: A five-part framework for powerful teaching and learning (grades K–6).* Teachers College Press.

Watson, R. (2019). *Some places more than others*. Bloomsbury Children's Books.

Winn, M. T., & Behizadeh, N. (2011). The right to be literate: Literacy, education, and the school-to-prison pipeline. *Review of Research in Education, 35*(1), 147–73.

Yopp, H. K., & Yopp, R. H. (2009). Phonological awareness is child's play. *Young Children, 64*(1), 12–21.

Zepeda, S. J. (2019). *Professional development: What works*. Routledge.

Index

Page references for figures are italicized

affirming, ix, xvii, xxi–xxvi, xxix, xxxii, 1, 3, 5, 7, 9–11, 30, 33–43, 45–49, 51–53, 57, 63
    educator, xxxii
    instruction, xxix, 1, 3, 5, 7
    language, xxx, 47
    lens, xxii, 34, 42, 45
    literacy instruction, xxix, xxxi, 38
    pedagogies, xxi
    and responsive, xxiii–xxiv, xxxi, 10, 33, 34, 45–47, 49, 52, 53, 57
    See also culturally affirm
antiracist, xxviii, 53, 55
art, xxx, 20, 22, 25, 32
assessment, xxiv, xxvii, xxix, xxxi, 15, 33–44, 46–49
Assessment as an Act of Love, 40
Assessment as inquiry, 34–37, *39,* 41, 43–44, 49
autonomy, xxvi, 3, 13, 35

barriers, xxx–xxxi, 2–3, 7, 9–11, 25, 34–35, 56
beliefs, xxiv, xxviii, xxix, xxxii, 5, 9, 35
bias(es), xx–xxii, xxiv, xxvii, 37, 42

collaborate, xxviii, 38, 45
colorblind, 6
Common Core State Standards (CCSS), 3
community, xii, xvii, xix, xx, xxi, xxii, xxvi, xxviii, xxx–xxxii, 8, 10–11, 13–14, 18–29, 31–32, 38, 41–42, 44–45, 48–49, 56
    assets, 18–19
    class(room), xvii, xix, 10
    educational, 8
    build(ing), xxvi, 11, 45, 48
conference, 36, 42, 44, 47
Covid-19, xxiii, 51
cultural, xxi, xxv, xxvii, xxix, xxxii, 4, 7, 16–19, 22, 35, 40, 45–48
    asset(s), 18
    identities, 4, 7
    knowledge, xxix, 17, 35, 45–48
    wealth, 16, 19
culture, xi, xix, xx, xvii, xxix, 4–7, 14, 17–19, 22–26, 28, 30–32, 35, 40, 47
    character's, 17
    popular, 7
    student's, 5
    supportive, 8
culturally affirm(ing), xxiii–xxiv, xxxi, 1, 5, 7, 10–11, 33–34, 45, 47, 49, 52–*53,* 57

Index

culturally responsive, xvii–xxii, 3–4, 6, 8–9, 11, 14, 17–18, 26, 29–32, 34–38, 40–41, 44–45, 48, 52, 56
    and affirming, xvii, xxi–xxii, xxix, xxxii, 3, 38, 41, 45, 63
    assessment, 34
    educator(s), xxvii–xxviii, 31
    framework, xx
    instruction, xvii–xix, xxiv, xix–xxx, 8, 14, 17–18, 29–31, 36, 56
    lens, xvii, xix, xxvi, xxviii, 34–35, 37
    materials, xxvi
    pedagogy, xxix, 3, 32
    spaces, xxiii
    strategies, xxxi
    teaching, xxix–xxxii, 3–4, 6, 11, 26, 60, 62
    texts, 18
curriculum/curricula, xiii, xvii–xviii, xxiv, xxvi–xxvii, xxix–xxx, xxxii, 2–7, 9, 11, 14–15, 26, 30, 34–36, 40, 53, 56
    evaluating, xxvi, 2
    literacy, 40
    materials, xxvi, xxix, 2, 15
    required, xxvi
    scripted, xxviii, 56

deficit, xii, xxii, xxv–xxvi, 5–7, 19, 42–43, 45–46
    language, xii, xxii, xxv, 45
    lens, xxvi, 42
    thinking, 42
diverse, xxix–xxx, 1, 3–4, 9–11, 14–15, 18–20, 26, 29–30, 53–54, 56
    books, 53
    communities, 19, 29
    perspectives, 18, 30
    student(s), xxix, 1, 3, 9
    texts, 4, 10, 15, 20
    topics, 18
    world, xxx, 11
diversity, xiii, xix, xxviii–xxx, 3, 15

equity, xxx–xxxi, 6–8, 11, 39–40, 52–53, 55
examine, xviii, xxiii, xxvii, 24, 32, 52

family, xx–xxii, 2, 6–7, 10, 18–19, 22–25, 27–28, 36–37, 47
feedback, xxvii, 38, 45
Floyd, George, xxiv, 51, 55
framework, xi, xx, xxiii–xxiv, xxvi, xxix, xxxi, 2, 9, 14–16, 18, 26, 30, 35, 37, 41, 44, 48–49, 53–55
    See also culturally responsive
funds of knowledge, xxiv–xxvi, 5, 14, 34, 45–47, 51

genre(s), 5, 14, 25–28, 36

identity, xii, xviii–xx, xxv–xxvi, xxix, xxxi–xxxii, 2–3, 11, 13–30, 32, 44, 46, 54, 56
    academic, xx
    connecting, xxix, xxxi
    explore, xxxi, 13, 21, 32
    gender, 3
    marginalized, xxix
    student, xxvi, xxxii, 18, 56
inclusive, xi, xxii, 38, 45–46, 53, 55–56
inequity, 55
injustice, xxii, 7, 51
inquiry cycle, *39*, 41, 43–44
interviews, xxvii, 23, 28, 41, 55
It's Not "One More Thing," xvii, *xxiii*

joy, xix, 16, 22, 32

K–12, xvii, xxi, xxix–xxxi, 2, 20, 37, 53, 55
kidwatching, 41, 44
    literacy, xii, xxii–xxiii, xxv, xxvi–xxxii, 2–4, 6–8, 13–14, 16, 20, 33–38, 40–42, 44–49, 52
    activity, 36
    assessment, xxix, xxxi, 33, 35, 37–41, 49
    behaviors, 36, 44

classroom, xxv
education, xxxii, 3, 37
educator(s), xxvii, 14, 48
engagement, 36
instruction, 37–38, 40, 46, 52
instructional decisions, 34–35, 37
interest, 37
knowledge, 35–37, 40, 42, 47
learning, xxv
lens, xxvii
methods, 4
practices, xi, xxxi, 6–7, 36
skills, xii, 36
standards, xxvii, 2, 20
strengths, 40, 45–46, 48
see also curriculum/curricula

marginalized, xvii–xviii, xxix, 7, 30, 32, 54–56
mentor text(s), 2, 13, 16, 20
middle grade, 22–23
middle school, xx, 13–14
mirrors, 4, 7, 15
music, xxx, 15, 22–23, 25–26, 28, 32, 37

narrative(s), xiii, xxxi, 2, 5–6, 13–14, 17–20, 23, 25–28

parent(s) xi, xx, xxi, xxviii, 3, 11, 30–31, 43
people of color, xvii, xxii
pedagogy, xii–xiii, xxiv, xxvii, xxix, 2–3, 6–9, 14–15, 30, 32, 40, 47
phonological awareness, 41
poem, 22, 24, 27
poetry, 23, 27–28, 36
prompt(s), xxxi–xxxii, 15, 18–24, 30, 36–38, 40, 42–48
    analysis, 45–46
    for students, 21–23
    writing, 15, 20–22, 24, 30, 42

racism, xix–xx, xxii–xxiv, 3, 51

representation, xxvii, 15, 25

sample texts:
    African American Art: Harlem Renaissance, Civil Rights Era, and Beyond, 25
    Alma and How She Got Her Name, 22
    Clap When You Land, 24
    Drop Me off in Harlem [song], 25, 27
    "Harlem," 25
    Harriet Tubman Memorial Stands as a Symbol of Fortitude and Freedom in Harlem, 60
    The History of Times Square, 25
    Indian No More, 23
    Manhattan [song], 25
    My Papi Has a Motorcycle, 21
    The Negro Speaks of Rivers, 25
    A New African American Identity: The Harlem Renaissance, 25
    The New Colossus, 25
    "Ode to Family Photographs," 24
    Some Places More Than Others, 20, 22, 23
    Welcome to New York [song], 25, 27
social action, xxviii, 32, 41
social change, xxiv, xxviii, xxxii, 9, 14, 26, 29–30
space(s), xviii–xx, xxii–xxiii, xxv, xxxi, 5–6, 11–12, 15, 19–20, 30, 33–35, 43, 45, 49, 52–54, 56
    create/creating, 12
    educational, 53–54
    harmful, xx
    home, 6
    learning, xxii
    make, xxi, 15, 19, 34–35, 49

opening, 5
provide, 19–20
safe, 53
unwelcoming, xx
spelling inventories, 41
story, 1–2, 4, 13, 16–17, 21–24, 27–28
storytelling, xxx, xxxi, 13, 18–22, 24, 26–30, 32
strengths–based, 30, 42, 45–46
students of color, xviii, xxiii, 6–7, 39, 52–55

teacher(s), xi–xiii, xix–xxi, xxiii, xxvi–xxviii, xxx–xxxi, 2–5, 7–10, 13–15, 19, 24, 32, 34–35, 37–42, 44, 46, 48–49, 52–53, 55, 57
   classroom, xix, xxi, 38, 44, 53
   culturally responsive, xxii, xxxi, 35, 40
   inservice, xxviii, 19
   mentor, 4
   practicing, 35, 37, 42, 48
   preservice, xxiii, xxviii, 4, 7, 19, 32, 37, 38, 44, 53
   student, xxi, 33

window(s), 4, 15, 49
writing, xvii, xxv, 1–3, 5–6, 13–27, 30, 32, 36, 41–42, 44, 46, 51–52, 55–56

About the Authors

Christy Howard has been an educator for more than twenty years. Her experience in K–12 education includes serving as a middle school ELA teacher, a district curriculum specialist, and an instructional support coach for beginning teachers. She is currently an associate professor in the Department of Literacy Studies, English Education, and History Education at East Carolina University, where she teaches undergraduate and graduate courses. In her free time, she enjoys traveling and spending time with her family.

Mikkaka Overstreet has been an educator since 2006 and earned her PhD in curriculum and instruction in 2015. She was an elementary school teacher for five years, before working as a literacy consultant for her state department of education. Previously, she was a literacy professor; now, she is a literacy specialist at an education nonprofit. In her spare time, Mikkaka writes fiction, reads, and spoils her partner and cats.

Anne Swenson Ticknor is a professor in the literacy education program at East Carolina University. She has been an elementary teacher, a district and state literacy specialist, and a teacher educator over her nearly thirty-year career in education. Her research interests continue to be focused on equity in education and centering marginalized voices through literacy. When not working, Anne swims, bikes, and cooks.

www.ingramcontent.com/pod-product-compliance
Lightning Source LLC
Chambersburg PA
CBHW021215240426
43672CB00026B/317